D1373216

Perpetual Jubilee:
Meditations on
the Chaldean Liturgical Year

Fr. Andrew Younan

Published by the Chaldean Media Center
Chaldean Media Center, 1627 Jamacha Way, El Cajon, CA, USA

www.kaldu.org

First Edition Published in San Diego in 2014

Cover design by Andrew Hermiz.

ISBN-13: 978-1497343672
ISBN-10: 1497343674

First Printing.

Table of Contents

Introduction

This book contains short reflections on what were traditionally called *'Onyatha d-Basalyqe*, the "Basilica Responsories," which is the name given to the "Proper," that is, specifically-chosen, hymns for Evening Prayer of each of the Sundays and Feast Days of the Chaldean Liturgical year. The purpose of these reflections is to reveal to the faithful of the Chaldean Church, or anyone interested in its spirituality, the great richness of that tradition, to show the depth of the theology contained in these hymns, and most of all to bring about a true devotion in the hearts of the reader, which is the purpose of all liturgy and all meditation. Thus there is a translation of these hymns for each Sunday and many major Feasts, accompanied by a meditation that helps explain the meaning of the hymn to the lay person with basic Catechetical education.

For the most part, these reflections were written as content for kaldu.org, the website of the Chaldean Catholic Diocese of St. Peter the Apostle. This book best accompanies the recently-published *Emmanuel* prayer book in giving devotional content to the liturgical prayers contained in that volume. For a scientific and historical explanation of the Chaldean liturgical year, see Chapter 2 of Mar Sarhad's Introduction to *Emmanuel.*

That Essay is the source of the title of this book. Early on, the Bishop quotes the book of Leviticus: "Seven weeks of years shall you count --seven times seven years-- so that the seven cycles amount to forty-nine years... **This fiftieth year you shall make sacred by proclaiming liberty in the land** for all its inhabitants. **It shall be a jubilee for you.**" (Leviticus 25:8-10). Concluding the Essay, he shows how the Chaldean Church fulfilled this Jubilee cycle of 7 x 7 in her liturgical year:

> This would be the adjusted Mesopotamian liturgical year, **a perpetual Jubilee**:
>
> 1. Subara: 4 weeks + Christmas Season (2 Sundays flexible)
> 2. Din<u>h</u>a: 7 weeks, flexible
> 3. <u>S</u>awma: 7 weeks
> 4. Qyamta: 7 weeks
> 5. Pentecost with Shly<u>h</u>e: 7 weeks
> 6. Purification=<u>H</u>allilayn: 7 weeks
> 7. <u>S</u>lywa: 7-10 weeks (including Elijah and Moses, flexible)
> Crown of the Year - Coronation of the Church: 4 weeks

Every year in our Christian age is a Jubilee year. Every year is a year of liberty and salvation.

Fr. Andrew Younan

The First Sunday of *Subara*

Hear, O Shepherd of Israel.

He who was before the ages.

God the Word, who is from the Father,

did not assume the form of a servant from the angels,

but rather from the seed of Abraham,

and came in our humanity, by his grace,

to save our race from error.

Silence

Silence is the beginning of spirituality. In order to have depth in his heart and know God intimately, man must dig beneath the surface of sight and sound around him, and search for the Spirit of God who dwells in his depths. This is not to say that God is not about him and only within, but in order to notice the Hidden One, the mind must focus, meaning it must exclude exterior, empty, shallow things and allow itself to notice only what God would point out. In other words, in order to hear God the Word speak to us, we must put all else aside and listen to him.

The first Basilica Hymn of the year begins with exactly this phrase: "**God the Word, who is from the Father.**" The Father expresses himself perfectly in his one Word, and if we are to know him it is through Christ, the Word made flesh. The rest of the hymn is dramatically simple:

God the Word, who is from the Father, did not assume the likeness of a servant from the angels, but rather from the seed of Abraham, and came in our humanity, by his grace, to save our race from error.

This hymn is the fruit of a long and silent meditation on the reality of the Incarnation. This is clear because of its form: there is no addressee, no petition, no "let us" conclusion to spur us on to activity. It is a simple statement of fact, and the author knows that it is enough, in this case, to simply state this fact. This is not the desperate prayer of one begging for God's aid and mercy; nor is it even spoken to God; nor is it an exhortation given to an earthly soul. The group addressed is universal, since it speaks of "our humanity." This hymn is therefore the spark, the light of insight given to a meditative mind after hours of silent listening, of the sensitive observance of the history of salvation.

Son of Man

What is the meaning of this common title given to the Lord Jesus Christ? Certainly it echoes many of the prophecies of the Old Testament, especially those of Ezekiel and Daniel, but is there something more primordial in this title? Our hymn refers to the Word incarnate in humanity as a contrast with other possibilities: "...**did not assume the form of a servant from the angels, but rather from the seed of Abraham**..." It was possible for the Creator to take any form he wanted, such as that of an angel; even in doing so he would have still taken the "**likeness of**

a servant," for angels serve at his throne as well. But he chose instead to become a son of Abraham, a man of a particular race chosen by God.

What does it mean to be man? What is this "humanity" assumed by the Son of God? The definitions are many, though the most widely accepted in philosophy is "rational animal." But this definition is so limited in its scope, and so incomplete. Scripture gives a deeper one: man is the image of God. This concept breaks away the boundaries we use to make our mind comfortable, and shows that we are well beyond our own comprehension, for if God is a mystery to us, our own nature shares in that mystery. An anonymous poet expresses this idea in the following way:

> Yet you have made him little less than God,
> This fleshy vehicle for sin and thought,
> For mind and lust. Now vicious (he would nod
> To sleep in minutes in that Heaven bought
> For him in Blood) and now a saint portrayed,
> And still his value known by increment:
> In sinfulness, at least in Likeness made;
> In saintliness, at most an instrument.
> In neither way his value undermined:
> No matter scope of sin, he cannot drag
> His dignity beneath his noble mind,
> But yet if good, unable still to brag.
> In any case, the lion and the lamb;
> In any case, the seed of Abraham.

Intimacy

Finally, the Incarnation is a mystery that, despite being beyond our slightest comprehension, is a reality that touches the depths of our being. It was not any conceptual humanity that was assumed by the Son of God, but a real, particular, flesh-and-blood human *Qnoma* (individualized nature) one like us in all things but sin. The liturgy of the Church of the East is therefore fond of calling it "**our humanity**," showing the depth of the union between God and man in Jesus Christ, who brings God to earth and man to heaven.

The Second Sunday of *Subara*

He who was before the ages.

His Name was before the sun.

The great Mystery that had been hidden for centuries and for generations has been revealed to us in the final age: the Only-Begotten One, who is in the Womb of his Begetter, came and assumed the form of a servant in his grace; and he related and revealed to us the perfect faith of the Trinity.

Suspense

God, the Author of history, works in ways we understand; he writes in our language, because we are his audience. If we understand this well, we can make sense of his action in our world. Salvation history, as presented perfectly in the Scriptures, is the story of how God speaks to us and, gradually and by degrees, brings us to a greater knowledge of himself. As a human author utilizes every technique to relate a truth to his reader, and adapts himself as his audience requires, so God makes use of the many kinds of human expression to reveal the ultimate Truth, who is Jesus Christ.

But a Truth this sublime cannot be told, in human language, in a single sentence. It required centuries of preparation beforehand, in Moses and the Prophets, before this full expression could even begin, and even afterward it has taken centuries for us to begin to understand what was revealed in Christ – and this only with the help of the Holy Spirit. This long preparation and post-interpretation is necessary – there is no way God could have revealed himself so fully without shaking the world both before and after.

This "divine suspense" in our waiting for the Lord's manifestation in the flesh is a fruitful exercise in spirituality, since it is precisely what prepares us for receiving him when he comes. It also reminds us how special we are in being of the "generation" of those to whom he was revealed, that is, the generation of believers. The second Basilica Hymn of the liturgical year says it thus:

> **The great Mystery that had been hidden for centuries and for generations has been revealed to us in the final age...**

The Method

How then did God finally show what he wanted to show? The "**final age**" is the age begun by the Incarnation of Christ, the Son of God. The "pedagogical method" of God, then, is in taking flesh, becoming man, becoming one of his students, in order to teach them more directly:

...the Only-Begotten One, who is in the Womb of his Begetter, came and assumed the form of a servant in his grace...

The humility of a servant, which is what is shown in the example of the Only-Begotten, is the necessary classroom in which the ultimate lesson of Divinity is taught. Without this humility, which the Word of God showed us by example, the Mystery can never be known.

The Mystery

What then is this great Mystery? What is it which God revealed in Christ, after centuries and generations of preparation and waiting?

...and he related and revealed to us the perfect faith of the Trinity.

The three *Qnome* of the Father, Son and Holy Spirit in one God is the ultimate, salvific Mystery which was prepared for by all the prophets and which has been reflected upon for centuries. This is the reason Christ came; knowing this Truth is our salvation. It is knowing God with this kind of intimacy and living with him so closely that gives our life meaning and truth.

The Third Sunday of *Subara*

My heart overflows with noble words.

His Name was before the sun.

He who is neither understood nor limited by creatures has accomplished his plan in our humanity: indeed, the divine Nature has united to the human nature he has assumed, while not changing. The Virgin gave birth in holiness to Christ, the Power of God and his Wisdom. While adoring, we all confess Him to be one Son who is the Savior of the world.

New Wine

The heaviness of our daily routine can make it easy for us to slouch spiritually, to see the world with aged eyes and, worst of all, to become bored with the life that God has given us. Qoheleth the prophet takes up the voice of just such a one when he writes, with great poignancy, the following verses:

> Vanity of vanities, says Qoheleth,
>
> vanity of vanities! All things are vanity!
>
> What profit has man from all the labor
>
> which he toils at under the sun?
>
> One generation passes and another comes,
>
> but the world forever stays.
>
> The sun rises and the sun goes down;
>
> then it presses on to the place where it rises...

All speech is labored;

there is nothing man can say.

The eye is not satisfied with seeing

nor is the ear filled with hearing.

What has been, that will be;

what has been done, that will be done.

Nothing is new under the sun. (Ecclesiastes, 1:2-5, 8-9)

Being so dark, this is cannot be the last word. The Lord himself, speaking through the prophet Isaiah, brings hope out hopelessness as he created light out of darkness and being from nothingness: "See, I am doing something new! Now it springs forth, do you not perceive it? In the desert I make a way, in the wasteland, rivers." (Isaiah 43:19).

We may be bored with the world, but God is certainly not; for us, the possibilities may have been exhausted, but never for him. Out of deserts and wastelands he can make living waters flow. But in spiritual matters this transformation and rejuvenation requires our cooperation, since it is our will, our heart, which is renewed. This is what Christ means when he says "neither is new wine put into old wineskins; if it is, the skins burst, and the wine is spilled, and the skins are destroyed; but new wine is put into fresh wineskins, and so both are preserved." (Matthew 9:17). That is, if a new element is to enter into an old situation, whatever is old must become new; if Christ, who is ever new, is to enter our lives, we must become new ourselves, or we will burst.

And not only new, but totally, completely new. The reason for this is because the "new wine" in this case is not something which simply expands with air as it ferments, but which is absolutely expansive; the One who has no limitation or boundaries himself wishes to dwell within us, within "our humanity," and we must stretch out our souls and be stretched out to infinity if we are to become his temples. The Person of Christ shows this perfectly, as he is the First-Born of the New Creation:

> **He who is neither comprehended nor limited by creatures has accomplished his plan in our humanity: indeed, the divine Nature has united to the human nature he has assumed, while not changing.**

If this is the case, then one of two things must happen: the humanity of Christ, and in some sense "our humanity" in which it partakes, must be obliterated in being united to the pure eternal Fire of Divinity, or it must be "united" and "assumed." The latter is obviously the case: for the human *Qnoma* of Christ, union with God and existence itself occur at the same moment, and the latter is in fact an effect of the former.

Unity

The grace of God is a powerful reality, one which is all-pervading and all-powerful. In every case, its purpose is to unite God and man. In the case of the God-Man Jesus Christ, however, the union of two *Qnome* is not a result of grace but rather the cause of grace in every man. Thus while our union with God through the grace of Christ is something that can increase and decrease, something that depends on our faith, our participation in the sacraments, our good works, etc., Christ becomes himself, from the moment of his conception until now, the permanent and unquenchable fount of grace for the whole human race.

That is why it is right to call Jesus Christ unreservedly "the Power of God" and "the Wisdom of God," because of the perfect and absolute union between the two natures in his Person:

The Virgin gave birth in holiness to Christ, the Power of God and his Wisdom. While adoring, we all confess Him to be one Son who is the Savior of the world.

The Fourth Sunday of *Subara*

His lightning lights up the world.

At the edge of the sky is his departure.

The Splendor of the Father who was revealed from the house of David in our humanity has been seen: he reigns over those of the house of Jacob, and there is no end to his authority. An angel announced to Mary; he gave a greeting full of mercies to the Virgin, and announced a hope full of blessings to the holy woman: "Peace be with you, blessed among women, full of hope! Peace be with you, and blessed are you, giver of birth without copulation! For from you will dawn the Lord of height and depth and all within them! To him be glory from every mouth!" O Lord, glorious is the day of your annunciation!

A Veil?

In a certain radical way, everything we say about God is wrong. That is, none of the words we use can encapsulate his Essence completely, or even signify something about him with total accuracy. When we say "God is good," we know it is true, but we also know that it cannot be true in the same way that we normally use the word "good," because God's goodness is not only completely beyond any created goodness, but somehow even a goodness of a completely different kind. We also say that "pizza is good." It is impossible that the same adjective can be used, in the

12

same way, to describe God's goodness, even if it is made ultra-superlative. It is not accurate to say "God is good in the way that pizza is good, but much, much better." No, God's goodness is of a totally different order, one connected analogically to our language but utterly beyond it in itself.

This is all quite abstract, but its concrete application becomes very interesting when Christ comes into the picture. Christ is the Word of this same God made flesh. He is the One who is utterly beyond our language and our understanding who is expressed and expresses himself in our humanity. How is this so? How can it be that the Light of God, which is so bright that it would blind us, become visible before our very eyes?

There are necessarily two approaches to this question, both found in the tradition of the Church of the East within her own hymns and prayers. The first may be summarized by this stanza taken from the Basilica Hymn of Christmas Day, one of the handful that is not extant in the Chaldean Breviary:

> *It was not that the Existence became flesh in the womb, as you suppose, who are deaf to reasoning. It was a dwelling which he chose for himself to hide his Radiance, that the mortal race might not perish in seeing him.*

This stanza presents us with several problems. First, it contradicts the inspired terminology of Scripture when it denies the validity of saying "became flesh." Second, it is clearly polemic, addressing those who are "deaf to reasoning," and it is doubtful that such a tone and address are appropriate in the Church's public prayer to God.

Still, is there something valid here? Is there some point that is worth making theologically? It was said to Moses that no one may see God and live (Exodus 33:20). Even in the Person of Christ, when he was walking upon the earth, what was seen in seeing him was his humanity, not his Divinity directly.

The question becomes, therefore, what is the function of Christ's humanity? Is it, as this stanza suggests, to veil his Divinity, lest we see God's pure Light and perish? Is the job of Christ's humanity to hide God? Or is it something else?

The Medium

The Basilica Hymn for the Fourth Sunday of Advent presents us another picture of the role of Christ's humanity, which in its nature is identical to our own:

The Splendor of the Father who was revealed from the house of David in our humanity has been seen: he reigns over those of the house of Jacob, and there is no end to his authority.

In itself and directly, the Light of God is too bright for us to see – which metaphorically means that as a Spirit, God is not of a nature that is visible to physical eyes like ours.

But what if God himself were to make his Light shine in a way that was visible to us? What if there were a medium, a meeting-point between the spectrum of human life and the infinite brightness of God? This is the function of the humanity of Christ.

Christ is the meeting-point, the Medium, in Biblical terms the Mediator, between God and man; he presents each one to the other in their own respective understandings. To God he presents a humanity sinful but forgiven in his Blood and alive in him; to man he shows a God come down to talk to them face to face. Christ is the translator between the language of God and that of man; his humanity takes the One Uncreated Word which expresses the Fullness of God and makes it audible to us as we are accustomed to hearing.

Sources

Finally, we need to analyze an abrupt shift in the tone and content of our hymn. There is an immediate turn, without even a word of transition, from speaking of the "Splendor of the Father" and his authority on earth to the event of the annunciation to Mary by the angel:

An angel announced to Mary; he gave a greeting full of mercies to the Virgin, and announced a hope full of blessings to the holy woman: "Peace be with you, blessed among women, full of hope! Peace be with you, and blessed are you, giver of birth without copulation! For from you will dawn the Lord of height and depth and all within them! To him be glory from every mouth!" O Lord, glorious is the day of your annunciation!

Five times in these lines is the root "sbar" used in various ways and translated here as "announced," "hope," and "annunciation." The hope of the human race's re-union with God exists in the Person of Christ, who is both God and man. But as the Son of God, he is not the Source of Divinity – that is reserved for the Father; and as the Son of man, the source of his humanity is Mary.

The Holy Feast
of the Birth of Our Lord

There I will make a horn to sprout for David.

In the flesh was born,

from the house of David,

Christ our Life-Giver,

whose birth gladdened all.

The Lord of glory

is from the Father

and in human flesh:

Christ, the seed of Abraham.

From those who walk in innocence.

Christ the Lord was born

of the Virgin Mary,

and is of the seed

of David and Abraham.

His Majesty's power

is placed in his hand;

his authority

rules heaven and earth.

Praise him and sing to him.

Angels glorified,

and their ranks cried out:

"Glory in heaven,

and peace upon earth!"

The whole mortal race

sang and glorified,

in the birth of Christ,

who has saved our race.

From then the nations will praise with him.

Nations and gentiles,

come and glorify

Jesus Christ the Lord

who has saved our race,

turned our ignorance

to the light of truth,

and gave us, in grace,

his eternal life.

He will be like a tree planted near a stream of water.

The Fruit of Gladness

dawned from Mary's womb;

he forgave our sins

and erased our debts.

He came, searched for us,

raised our death to life,

and renewed our race

that had drowned in sin.

Gladness over all the earth.

At the birth of Christ,

the angels proclaimed:

"Glory in heaven

and peace upon earth."

O mortals, come now,

take the bond of sin,

the Fruit of Mary's womb

has redeemed our race.

The Most Important Things

The reflections found in the Basilica Hymns, and in all the spiritual heritage of the Church of the East, profound as they are, are deeply humble in their self-understanding. Though they are about the loftiest Divine things, the authors are human, and their reflections and writings are those of human beings.

One so self-conscious of his humanity will therefore take a step back when it comes to the deepest things, and realize his limitation in explaining them. The Basilica Hymns of the Feast of the Birth of Our Lord are not theological reflections but simply poetical discourses on the reality they are celebrating. This is one of the cases when it is somehow too much to say anything more than what has been said.

The Memorial

of the Blessed Virgin Mary

Our God, our mighty stronghold.

He has chosen a dwelling for himself.

The daughter of man became the Tree of Life for the whole mortal race, for the Glorious Fruit which dawned from her pours forth and grants all benefits. Come, O mortals, let us be brought near to the sweetness of his words, and sing praise to him!

The Tree of Life

It is impossible, or at least ridiculous, to imagine the nativity scene without Mary. Though she is not, and never is, the central figure, she is totally essential to the scene, and she is the closest to the One who is the central figure, Christ the newborn. This being the case, the richness of the image guides our eyes, our line of sight, from one thing to another: the angel points us to the cave; the cave points us to what is inside; the shepherd visitors inside point, with their glances, to the middle of the cave where three central characters sit; Joseph is faithfully protecting Mary; and Mary, with her loving eyes and tender hands, with every speck of her being, is pointing to her Son.

This perfect balance in imagery must be here in this re-construction of the family, but such harmony is not always there in human realities. It was certainly not there at the family's destruction. No such balance was to be found when Adam and Eve sinned against God; there the pointing is not one of meaning, but of accusation, the sequence not one of importance, but of blame. God points to Adam in condemnation; Adam points to Eve and back to God whom he blames for her creation; Eve points to the serpent. There is no center in this scene, no balance, no harmony; everything is backwards.

Adjacent to this scene of condemnation in the third chapter of Genesis there is another scene, forgotten and left behind in the mess and chaos caused when Adam and Eve realized they were naked. The parallel scene is a quieter one, though equally tragic: it is a scene of two trees. One tree, meant to be untouched, is mutilated: the serpent's filthy tracks may still be imprinted upon it; a fruit is torn off against the command of God, eaten and shared; most likely, it was dropped next to the tree by the perpetrators in their fear, with only those two fatal bites taken from it; very likely, its leaves were ripped away and used for clothing by the parents who gave birth both to the whole human race as well as to its shame.

The second tree, more important but further in the background in this twisted play, is protected, guarded by force from the thieves who stole what was not rightfully theirs. The Tree of Life is forgotten in the scramble by all but God, who knows the real meaning and importance of everything in the garden. More important even than the Tree of Life, however, and so forgotten by the ungrateful race of men that it is barely mentioned by the author of Genesis, is the Fruit of Life that the tree produces. What is to become of this tree and its fruit? For whom were they made, and to what purpose?

The Tree of Life, in the tradition of the Church of the East, has two fulfillments: the ultimate one is the Cross of Christ, which carried the One who is to be eaten, who is to dwell within us and give us life everlasting. But the first Tree of Life, from whom the Fruit of Life was produced, is Mary:

The daughter of man became the Tree of Life for the whole mortal race, for the Glorious Fruit which dawned from her pours forth and grants all benefits. Come, O mortals, let us be brought near to the sweetness of his words, and sing praise to him!

The Memorial of
the Murder of the Infants

Hear this, all you peoples

Come and see the works of God

Herod had schemed to kill the Son of God, and so he sent the magi kings with an evil intent and a hard heart. But, providentially, they did not return on their path, and went to their land by another way. When the fox saw their mockery, he was enraged against the Son of their Lord. He sent the head soldiers and murdered the infants. But lo, he is tortured in anguish, and they are delighting in the kingdom of heaven.

Glory to the Father and to the Son and to the Holy Spirit.

"Rachel weeps for her children, and does not want to be comforted," the glorious prophet, son of Helaqya, anticipated and declared, inspired by the Spirit, for he saw the infants and the children who were sacrificed and killed by the impure Herod, the one filled with evil, who desired to destroy the Only Begotten Son of Existence. Glory to him who became small while nothing was impossible for him, and who moved to Egypt, not for fear of the savage one, but for the fulfillment of prophecy.

Justice

It is a corruption to associate revenge with a sense of true justice. A just punishment given to one who deserves it is not the same thing as releasing an individual anger in a violent way to an object of anger. In the political sphere, the sense of justice, of one truly deserving punishment for his crime, is nearly lost. In the case of most incarcerations, the justification for the prison time is either to teach a lesson through rehabilitation or to protect society from a dangerous person. Though both of these justifications are excellent and rightly in their place, there is a very important missing element, and that is justice itself. Rehabilitation and public protection aside, certain crimes deserve, objectively and truly, certain punishments because of the nature of the act. To say otherwise is to declare arbitrary every moral code – what other way is there to say that something is really "wrong" other than saying it is "worthy of punishment?" Justice is thus hanging on by a thread in our world.

Certain crimes, however, go beyond an ordinary human sense of injustice, and are said to "cry out to heaven" for their recompense. Such a crime was the killing of the children done by Herod. The Basilica Hymn memorializing this event begins thus:

Herod had schemed to kill the Son of God, and so he sent the magi kings with an evil intent and a hard heart. But, providentially, they did not return on their path, and went to their land by another way. When

the fox saw their mockery, he was enraged against the Son of their Lord. He sent the head soldiers and murdered the infants. But lo, he is tortured in anguish, and they are delighting in the kingdom of heaven.

If there is any symbol of rage and false revenge, it is Herod. In order to thwart a practically imaginary foe (for Christ did not come to take over any earthly reign), he destroyed the lives of hundreds of innocent children and their families. The final line of the hymn shows that, in the end, there is an ultimate Justice meted out by God, the Just Judge.

Providence

Still, one must ask the question why this entire event happened at all? Why was it necessary for Herod to commit such a deed, and for God to allow it? Why was such suffering allowed?

"Rachel weeps for her children, and does not want to be comforted," the glorious prophet, son of Helaqya, anticipated and declared, inspired by the Spirit, for he saw the infants and the children who were sacrificed and killed by the impure Herod, the one filled with evil, who desired to destroy the Only Begotten Son of Existence. Glory to him who became small while nothing was impossible for him, and who moved to

Egypt, not for fear of the savage one, but for the fulfillment of prophecy.

Rachel refuses comfort. Even the promise of delight for her children and torture for their killer does not take away or undo the pain she feels at that terrible moment. This is a darkness that is not removed by the promise of a future light, a night that is not given meaning, during its duration, by the anticipation of the dawning day.

No explanation could have been given to those childless mothers as they tore their hair with their hands and their lungs with their screaming. Such is the nature of the most awful tragedies – their meaning is beyond the understanding both of any individual and of humanity as a whole. Its purpose in the Divine Plan, its allowance by God for some greater, unseen good, is not for us to explain or grasp, but only to accept and trust.

The First Sunday after Christmas

I will exalt you, O Lord God, my King
As is your Name, O Lord, so be your praises
O Lord, who is like you?
He who is in God's likeness, which is unseen.

O Lord of all, while you are in the likeness of God, you assumed the likeness of a servant in your love, and you neither robbed your Divinity nor defrauded your humanity. Rather, in both natures you are truly one Son, undivided. Indeed, above you exist without a mother, from the Father; and below, without a father, from a mother. Thus have the prophets anticipated and predicted; thus also have the apostles preached; and thus have the Fathers taught in the Church: so that, by their pleading and in their faith, you may protect us, O God, and have mercy on us.

Communication

Theology as an intellectual discipline has failed if it ever becomes entirely abstract. That is, its goal is not only, like other sciences, knowledge of its object of study but also, and most importantly, friendship with God. Studying the faith, the Scriptures, the tradition of the Church, the Fathers, the sacred liturgy, cannot be simply ways to gather data or to improve our ideas about God; they must first and foremost be ways for us to encounter God in our hearts and minds.

Of course, as a way to encounter God, theology is quite fit for its job. Man is set apart from other earthly creatures by his mind, and he must, in some way or another, use his mind to its fullest capacity in his search for meaning, in his encounter with his Creator. In other words, in order to know God, it helps very much to know about God.

For this reason, Advent and the prayers we have examined have been suitable preparations for the physical, face-to-face encounter we have with God in the nativity scene where Christ was born. All four Basilica Hymns from Advent have been beautiful reflections on the reality of what took place in Bethlehem so long ago. But all of them have known their place, for the actual encounter has, liturgically, not yet happened; "before" Christ is born in the liturgical year, none of the four hymns have addressed him. That honor is reserved for the hymn we examine now:

O Lord of all, while you are in the likeness of God, you assumed the likeness of a servant in your love, and you neither robbed your Divinity nor defrauded your humanity.

Balance

Again theologically, the whole issue is how this child is both God and man; but a clarification of terminology and definition of doctrine are but a first step, albeit a necessary one, to a true life of grace and prayer. In other words, if Christ is our salvation and the Mediator between God and man, if it is in knowing him that we know the Father and tread the path to heaven, it is of the highest importance that we know who he is. This is why heresy is such an evil thing; false teaching about who Christ is was condemned so dramatically by the Church because we cannot pray to Christ if we have a false idea of who he is, if we are worshiping an idol we have made in our minds rather than the one true living God.

Thus it is appropriate that this first "breakthrough" between the ideas of Advent and the direct prayer of the Christmas season return again, after its address, to the Mystery if Christ's Divine and Human identity:

Rather, in both natures you are truly one Son, undivided. Indeed, above you exist without a mother, from the Father; and below, without a father, from a mother.

A Personal Relationship

A curious division has taken place in the last few centuries between the individual and society. It has become believable somehow that a person can exist apart from others, or that he has the right to do so. This unnatural view on man, of whom God said that "it is not good for him to be alone," has seeped even into Christian spirituality. By some acrobatic feat of the imagination, it has become plausible to believe that one can worship Christ in isolation from the rest of the Church – meaning not that one can "go into his room" and pray to God as an individual member of the Church, but that Christ can be encountered and even defined apart from or even against the entire society to whom he was revealed in the beginning, which is the Church. Thus it is said that no association with the Body of Christ is necessary, but ONLY a "personal relationship" with him, as if one can exist without the other.

That Christ was prepared for by an entire nation is forgotten; that he was born to a woman of this nation; that he preached not to one individual but to many; that he was revealed as risen to a group (even Mary Magdalene was immediately told to tell the others); that this group preached his Lordship as a unified whole; that the Scriptures are the result of this preaching; that the Faith has always been the Faith of the Body of Christ and not of one member; all of these realities have been pushed aside without any valid justification.

Even if one has, unnaturally, made himself an island apart from others, Christ is not an island. He is connected to every member of his Body, and every member of his Body is connected to him and to every other member:

> **Thus have the prophets anticipated and predicted; thus also have the apostles preached; and thus have the Fathers taught in the Church: so that, by their pleading and in their faith, you may protect us, O God, and have mercy on us.**

The Second Sunday after Christmas

He will sprout from his city like the grass of the earth.
A comely and lovely plant; it produces leaves and forms almonds.
As is the staff of Aaron, which blossomed, so is the Virgin who conceived, O unbelieving Jew! That which was neither planted nor watered, sprouted; the Virgin, then, without husband and seed conceived by the command of God. The staff showed a wonderful Fruit; and the Power of the Most High came and rested upon her who is full of grace, and promised that she would give birth to Jesus Christ, the Savior of the world, whom we adore and to whom we say: Great, O Lord, is the mystery of your gracious providence; glory to you!

Precedence & Novelty

God is at once eternally ancient and ever new; he existed from eternity, before time began, and yet he has not aged a day, but is the constant Source of vitality and renewal. Thus are also all his works - while being always unexpected wonders, surprises which we could never have guessed, they have been prepared for from the beginning of salvation history. Thus while Christ's death for the sins of the world was a completely new reality, God prepared for it - that is, he prepared the mind of man to understand and accept it - by establishing a context for it, namely, here, a context of temple and sacrifice in which lambs and other animals were slain. This reality was in turn prepared for by the sacrifice of Isaac during which he asked his father Abraham, "Where is the lamb for the sacrifice?" Throughout every moment, every significant even of history, God is preparing to do something ever greater, and this all culminates in the person of Jesus Christ.

But Christ, like all men, is not an island; he also is found within a context, within a family, and all those surrounding him are affected by all that affects him. And so, they also are prepared for; they also are given a precedent in a way similar to Christ himself. Thus John the Baptist was announced by the prophet: "a voice crying out in the wilderness;" thus the Gentiles who heard Christ's preaching were made known to us: "the people who sit in darkness have seen a great light;" thus even Judas the betrayer was hinted at in Psalm 41: "even my close friend, whom I have trusted, who ate my bread, has risen his heel against me."

Intimacy

During this Christmas season, we gaze into the scene of the nativity of Christ, and it is there that we realize that because Christ is central, Mary is as well; if he is the middle of the scene, Mary is all around him; she is herself his context. How then could it be possible for Mary also to not have some preparation in salvation history? We hear the Gospels quoting the prophet

Isaiah, "a virgin shall conceive and bear a Son." This is an announcement; but the Fathers of our Church point out to us a mystical symbol as well, in order to answer an intellectual objection against this possibility, even this reality, that a virgin should be with child and give birth to the Savior of the world:

As is the staff of Aaron which blossomed, so is the Virgin who conceived, O unbelieving Jew! That which was neither planted nor watered, sprouted; the Virgin, then, without husband and seed conceived by the command of God. The staff showed a wonderful Fruit; and the Power of the Most High came and rested upon her who is full of grace, and promised that she would give birth to Jesus Christ, the Savior of the world, whom we adore and to whom we say: Great, O Lord, is the mystery of your gracious providence; glory to you!

The Holy Feast
of the Dawning of Our Lord

Come, let us bless and adore him.

We your people and the sheep of your flock.

We adore your holy dawning, O Lord, which has gladdened us, for in it, by a wonder, you enlightened all the nations who sat in darkness and in the shadow of death. O Lover of mankind, glory to you!

Come, let us praise the Lord.

Come, let us give thanks to Christ in whose revelation has freed us from error, has reconciled us with the Father by the oblation of his Body, and has pacified the exalted ones with us, who were enraged because of our wickedness. To him be glory, with his Sender!

The Perfect Summary

Just as in many Feasts of the highest importance, the Basilica Hymn of the Holy Feast of Dinha, or the Dawning of our Lord, is comprised of many verses reflecting on the events that have taken place for our salvation as well as the spiritual results of these events. It is probable that the multitude of these verses in the original *Hudhra* was sung during a procession, most likely from the Bema to the Sanctuary, where, after Ramsha was completed, Communion was given to the People of God.

The event of the Baptism of the Lord in the Jordan stands out as the beginning of his earthly, public ministry, but especially as the great "Dawning," the "Epiphany," the shedding of Light upon a world steeped in the darkness of ignorance. This is because God, in his most intimate Being, was revealed to the world at the Baptism of the Lord, and this revelation of the Essence of the Creator pointed back to the works of Christ on earth, specifically to his passion, death and resurrection.

Every element of the Faith is thus represented in the Baptism of the Lord: the Incarnation, in Christ's person and his conversation with John the Baptist; the Trinity, for the first time being revealed in the Son who was baptized, the Spirit who descended like a dove and the Voice of the Father praising his Son; even the redemption given through Christ is hidden in this marvelous event, since the baptism of the Church is one in Christ's death.

Let us proceed, therefore, in this procession; let us sing the songs of the Church to Christ on this holy day, and enter the Sanctuary as we sing. We enter a new liturgical season, one revealing the love of God anew in itself, and pointing with brightness to the very sacrifice of Christ.

The First Sunday of *Dinha*

Remember your Church, whom you chose from the beginning.
That through the Church, the manifold Wisdom of God
might be made known.

To your Church, O Savior, who has followed you perfectly by love and the faith which comes from baptism, you first showed the Qnome of glorious Divinity; and through her, the perfect teaching of the mystery of the Trinity was revealed to the spiritual assemblies. By your grace, O Lord, may the creed that has been delivered to her by you in your Gospel be preserved without stain.

Angels

There are many names for angels in the Christian tradition. The word "angel" itself means simply "messenger," and thus John the Baptist is called *angelos* in the Gospels. Under this aspect, angels are those who are sent by God from heaven for the sake of someone on earth. They are the guides, we are the guided; they are the teachers; we are the students.

In the Chaldean tradition, angels are sometimes called "Watchers" (*'yre*) and this name refers to the fact that they are unsleeping, and constantly awake, gazing at the glory of God and awaiting his commands.

37

Simply to use the word "spirits" is to name the angels according to the nature of their substance rather than according to any function, such as "angel/messenger" and "watcher."

Angels are also given categories such as "Cherubim" and "Seraphim," "Principalities" and "Powers." St. Paul refers to the latter two categories in the letter to the Ephesians: "through the Church the manifold wisdom of God might now be made known to the principalities and powers in the heavenly places." (3:10) These names refer to the glory of the angels, their headship and spiritual might.

Teachers & Students

Not surprisingly, all the names used for angels suggest, or even define strictly, that they are far superior to human beings. Human beings sleep; thus we cannot be "Watchers" in the same sense as angels; we are not always sent as messengers of God; we are not simple spirits but are embodied; nor are we heads of spiritual assemblies as Principalities or as powerful as Powers.

But in one sense we are superior to the angels - not in our nature as human beings, nor alone, but as a Church. Because of the Incarnation, Christ who is God and man (not angel) has united our nature with the Nature of the Godhead. This is literally the case with his own human *Qnoma*; but mystically, all of us in the Church are united to God in a special and privileged way as members of the Body of Christ.

This mystical reality found its first expression perhaps in the revelation of the Holy Trinity during the Baptism of Christ in the Jordan: there, the Son who came up from the water, the Spirit who descended like a dove and the Father whose voice was heard, were revealed to the unsuspecting world. Not only this, but in the place where St. Paul was quoted earlier we find an even greater reality. Even the angels did not know about the *Qnome* of the Trinity before the Baptism of Christ! That means that it was because of the Church, who needed, for her salvation, Christ to become man and baptized, that the angels of heaven learned more about God:

To your Church, O Savior, who has followed you perfectly by love and the faith which comes from baptism, you first showed the *Qnome* of glorious Divinity; and through her, the perfect teaching of the mystery of the Trinity was revealed to the spiritual assemblies. By your grace, O Lord, may the creed that has been delivered to her by you in your Gospel be preserved without stain.

The Second Sunday of *Dinḥa*

Then he spoke in signs to his just ones.

Age unto age tells of your works.

O Lord, from the beginning, you spoke with our fathers in every partiality and every type, and you taught them to worship your hidden and secret Nature. In the Last Days, however, through your true Son, you spoke to our race, and through him you made known to us that your glorious Divinity is announced in three *Qnome*. To you do all the legions of angels and men, who have been renewed in Christ, lift up glory.

Many Preparations

It is an awful host who invites guests to a banquet unprepared; imagine guests who have spent time and effort readying themselves - scheduling a block of time to be there, picking out clothing, etc. - only to arrive at a dinner where no food is ready, where the room is a mess, where the host shows no concern for his own invitation! No, a decent host would spend hours preparing for his guests, making sure everything was ready on time.

God had spent millennia preparing the world for the coming of his Son; communicating with the people of old who built the tower of Babylon; speaking to Abraham, then to Moses, speaking through all the prophets, year after year, century after century softening the hearts of his people to accept their Messiah, their Savior. It was not a simple process, nor a one-time act, from the side of us creatures, but a prolonged effort, if it can be said, metaphorically, that God expends effort.

The Basilica Hymn for the Second Sunday of Epiphany begins with a quote from the letter to the Hebrews reflecting on this reality of God's ceaseless preparation and communication with his people before the coming of Christ:

O Lord, from the beginning, you spoke with our fathers in every partiality and every type, and you taught them to worship your hidden and secret Nature.

God's banquet is not a mere triviality, of course; it has a serious purpose: for man to serve and worship God correctly.

One Way

But this manifold communication of God in times past is just that - past. Now, instead of partial words uttered here and there for this particular time or that, he has spoken his final Word, who is Jesus Christ. After Christ, the Incarnation of the Word, God has nothing more to say.

The greatest marvel, however, is not that God can fully express himself in one Word (his perfect Divine Simplicity implies that), but rather that this Word became expressed in our very own human flesh. It was through the man Jesus Christ that the Word was made perfectly manifest, and through the Word, the whole Trinitarian Glory of the Godhead:

In the Last Days, however, through your true Son, you spoke to our race, and through him you made known to us that your glorious Divinity is announced in three *Qnome*. To you do all the legions of angels and men, who have been renewed in Christ, lift up glory.

The Third Sunday of *Dinḥa*

Come and praise the Lord.

Come and see the works of God.

Come and be amazed, my beloved, at that wise Creator who, when he saw that his work was being mocked by the insolent, sent his Beloved and assumed our image, and revealed and made known, in him, the mystery that had been hidden from ages and generations. By his hand he was expounded, like the voice of the prosperous worker. Therefore, O Lord, we cry out and say: O you who made peace with the ages by his dawning: Glory to you!

A Wondrous Invitation

Only the Gospel of John relates the story of Andrew and another Disciple (possibly John himself) first meeting Jesus through the testimony of John the Baptist, who names Jesus the "Lamb of God." The Gospel narrative continues:

The two disciples heard him say this, and they followed Jesus. Jesus turned, and saw them following, and said to them, "What do you seek?" And they said to him "Rabbi" (which means Teacher), "Where are you staying?" He said to them, "Come and see." - John 1: 37-39

What would it have been like to enter the very home of Jesus? What kind of house was it? Who else was living there with him? Perhaps Mary? What sort of furniture did it have? And art? How was it decorated? And what did it feel like to be there? None of these questions is answered by the Gospel, and perhaps rightly - perhaps it is right for us not to know these things, so that our wonder can pull us more strongly toward Christ.

A Spiritual House

The Basilica Hymn for the Third Sunday of Epiphany begins in the same way, with a similar invitation:

Come and be amazed, my beloved, at that wise Creator who, when he saw that his work was being mocked by the insolent, sent his Beloved and assumed our form, and revealed and made known, in him, the mystery that had been hidden from ages and generations.

Here it is the mystery of salvation, and precisely the salvation that comes about in knowing the Trinitarian Nature of God, to which we are invited. Wonder is again the main emotion drawing us to **"be amazed"** at the Creator who was not satisfied simply with creating.

God is inviting us to be close to him not simply as the Creator, but as the Father, Son and Holy Spirit. God wants us not only to be his servants, but also members of his Divine Family; and so he becomes one of us and in his baptism and ours, opens up his front door and invites us in. That being the case, we who are baptized are now considered as adopted sons through Christ, and not only workers of the Kingdom of God:

By his hand he was expounded, like the voice of the prosperous worker. Therefore, O Lord, we cry out and say: O you who made peace with the ages by his dawning: Glory to you!

The Fourth Sunday of *Dinha*

How good and how pleasant.

Radiance and glory are before him.

Glorious and beautiful was the day of your birth, O Savior, and pleasant and excellent also the feast of your Epiphany, O Christ our Life-Giver. At your birth, O Lord, the sheepfold and the cave, the crib and the swaddling clothes, the star and the magi, the shepherds and the angels, all served in reverence. At your great and honorable Epiphany, John served in fear, and the river Jordan announced your baptism; the Father with his voice, and the Holy Spirit by his hovering, witnessed, O Lord, to your Divinity. We also glorify you: have mercy on us, O God!

Comparing Positives

It is possible to compare "good" to "bad," and in the category of human actions, that is the most fundamental comparison – some of our actions are "good" by their nature, and some are "bad." They are "good" when their object, as well as their means, are proportioned correctly to our happiness, and they are "bad" when this proportion is off. For example, our object can be "nourishing our bodies," and so we eat, but if this is done in the wrong way, say with unhealthy or excessive food, the act of eating can be "bad," because it does not lead to our happiness.

God's actions are not as ours. All is good within God, and it is utter blasphemy to attempt to categorize his actions as "good" or "bad," because all he does is perfect, both in its object (since all he does is for our ultimate perfection and happiness) and in its manner (since he does all in the most perfect way). Perhaps, however, the actions of God can be compared as "good" to "better," not from his perspective (since all is One in God), but from ours.

Because

What is the right way to understand the acts of God in relation to us? It should go without saying that those acts preparing for the Incarnation (basically the entire Old Testament) were done *for the sake* of the Incarnation, and for that very reason, the Incarnation is greater. Indeed, Aristotle supplies this as a maxim: "that for the sake of which is the greater." If this is our guiding principle, then we can move forward in our comparison. Whichever act is the *reason for* the other is the *greater*. The "because" is best, and everything tied to this "because" is good.

The Basilica Hymn for the Fourth Sunday of Epiphany makes a comparison like this between the Feasts of Christmas and Epiphany:

Glorious and beautiful was the day of your birth, O Savior, and pleasant and excellent also the feast of your

Epiphany, O Christ our Life-Giver. At your birth, O Lord, the sheepfold and the cave, the crib and the swaddling clothes, the star and the magi, the shepherds and the angels, all served in reverence. At your great and honorable Epiphany, John served in fear, and the river Jordan announced your baptism; the Father with his voice, and the Holy Spirit by his hovering, witnessed, O Lord, to your Divinity.

Comparing two good acts is one thing, but comparing two infinitely good acts is another entirely. Our author is stunned by both. On Christmas, he is amazed by the characters in the scene (the crib, the cave, the magi). This is impressive enough, but Epiphany is a different story. Here, John the Baptist – the greatest man born of woman, according to Christ - is the one who serves "in fear;" here it is not angels who cry out, but the Father himself; it is not the shepherds or the magi who witness to the event, but the Holy Spirit. It is for these reasons that in the earliest understandings of the liturgical year, Epiphany was considered far greater as a feast than Christmas.

The Fifth Sunday of *Dinḥa*

The earth was defiled with blood.

Their blood was spilled like water around Jerusalem, and there was no one to bury them.

The earth of Judah was defiled with the blood of children; but it was absolved by springs of water made holy. While Herod made the earth unclean by the murdering of children, you, O Lord, in your mercies, like the Good One, absolved the whole creation by your holy Epiphany. Great is your gift and your compassion, O Lord; glory to you!

The Horror

The Basilica Hymn for this Fifth Sunday of Epiphany recalls an event that occurred decades before the Baptism of our Lord, in the way someone might memorialize any terrible event in recent history: the slaughter of the innocents wrought by Herod shortly after the birth of Jesus. History has its way of imprinting itself upon our minds and imposing its meaning upon us, and this event must have left a scar upon the minds and hearts of those in the region:

The earth of Judah was defiled with the blood of children...

49

Blood in itself is tragic enough when it is spilled; the horror multiplies when it is the blood of a child. But while God does not force goodness into anyone's conscience, nor ever take away his freedom, he has the power to salvage the good that is left of his creation after we have at it, overturn the darkness that human sin spills upon his world, and even bring good out of evil:

...but it was absolved by springs of water made holy.

Rebirth

Somehow, the baptism of Christ overturned the slaughter of the innocents – and even more, as an element in the Redemption, it overturned all the evil in the world, to the ends of the earth. This is because the darkest of all evils, sin in the human heart, was conquered by Christ's passion and death, and it is in this passion and death that we participate when we are baptized:

While Herod made the earth unclean by the murdering of children, you, O Lord, in your mercies, like the Good One, absolved the whole creation by your holy Epiphany. Great is your gift and your compassion, O Lord; glory to you!

The gift of baptism given to us through Christ is the source of light in humanity, the light that banishes and undoes the darkness of sin in the world.

The Sixth Sunday of *Dinḫa*

And they will glorify your Name forever.

They will glorify you forever.

Above in the heights, all the legions of angels glorify you, and with you, your Father. On earth also, the whole race of mortals kneels before you and adores. For through the Jordan and the water in it, you sanctified all springs: you were baptized in it, while above sin, and showed us, in your mercy, the path of life's salvation. Thus were you pleased to free the whole race of mortals. O Lord, glory to you!

Above & Below

It is difficult, today, to present a clear picture of what exactly we mean when we say "heaven." In the ancient world, and indeed in most ancient languages, the word would have been the same as "sky," but no such simple physical association is possible any longer. Even in the ancient world, it would have been impossible, except in the most primitive culture, to conceive of God and the angels, or even of the "gods" of a pagan culture, living in the sky, somewhere physically "up." God is spirit, as are the angels, as even the gods became at a relatively early time in even pagan religions. Especially today, when "up" and "down" have become relative terms, and earth is no longer either the "bottom" or the "center" of any objectified space, heaven no more be conceived of as a location of any kind.

51

It must be the case, then, that heaven is not a location but a state of existence, a way of being, which is totally spiritual and beyond the confines of locality. Holiness, not vertical distance from the surface of the earth, is the standard for heavenliness, and it is most meaningful for us to understand heaven "above" in this way.

The Basilica Hymn of the Sixth Sunday of Epiphany plays with the images of up and down, of above and below:

Above in the heights, all the legions of angels glorify you, and with you, your Father. On earth also, the whole race of mortals kneels before you and adores.

Heaven being the "place" of the angels, and earth the place of human beings, the unification that occurs between the glorifications of the angels and the adoration of human beings is a striking one in the context of the sinful race of Adam. After the awful reality of sin, the human race was unworthy even of an earthly paradise, much less a heavenly one; and yet, because of some awesome event, this spiritual distance between heaven and earth is made nothing.

The Path of Humility

It is Christ who, through all that he did on this earth, shows us and is the one Path, the Way to heaven. It is not the construction of proud towers or the brute force of human will that unites us with the angels above, as in the construction of the tower of Babylon; it is not even looking "up" that points us in the right direction. On the contrary, it is looking down, it is the Incarnation, Christ, who is the very Humility of God, who accepted abjection and humiliation when he came down to this earth, which leads us up to the glorious, radiant light of heaven above:

For through the Jordan and the water in it, you sanctified all springs: you were baptized in it, while above sin, and showed us, in your mercy, the path of life's salvation. Thus were you pleased to free the whole race of mortals. O Lord, glory to you!

The Seventh Sunday of *Dinḫa*

I will exult you, O Lord, my King.

He who was before the ages.

The three *Qnome* of Existence were shown to us in the baptism of the Headship who is from us: the Mystery that had been hidden, in the Lord who was baptized, the Holy Spirit like the flesh of a dove which descended and rested upon the head of the Image from the house of David, and the Father who cried out and was shown to the onlookers: the amazing and wonderful approval. Blessed is he who, in his love, became a man, saved us, absolved us, and sanctified us in his baptism, and washed away our sins in his laver:

to him be glory!

Everything

The quest of philosophy has been, from the beginning, to understand and explain the world as a whole, rather than only some part of it. Whether or not any particular philosopher has been successful in doing this, or whether some have been more successful than others, is a question that perhaps no two people would answer in the same way. But when the Creator of this world, the Author of this hotly debated book of history, speaks for himself, the wise will listen.

The voice of the author was heard at the baptism of Christ, when the Father made himself heard and approved his Son, sending down his anointing Spirit to the Jordan river. This Trinitarian revelation burst open the mystery, the meaning, of everything that is, while at the same time keeping it a mystery:

> **The three *Qnome* of Existence were shown to us in the baptism of the Headship who is from us: the Mystery that had been hidden, in the Lord who was baptized, the Holy Spirit like the flesh of a dove which descended and rested upon the head of the Image from the house of David, and the Father who cried out and was shown to the onlookers: the amazing and wonderful approval.**

No amount of human speculation could have discovered the reality of the Trinitarian God; no amount of human reason, even that gifted with grace, could ever comprehend the meaning of the Father, Son and Holy Spirit in one Divine Godhead. This is a mystery where the solution is more stunning than the question.

Reaction

Unlike the vast majority of philosophers, however, the Christian faith is not satisfied with speculation, or even the possession of theoretical truth; it is not enough to know – our very life must change. Thus the revelation of the Trinity was at an event that points back to us and to our lives. When Christ was baptized, he showed us our need for cleansing; he showed us his closeness to our lowliness; he showed us the path of humility; and in showing us all of these things, he showed us God:

Blessed is he who, in his love, became a man, saved us, absolved us, and sanctified us in his baptism, and washed away our sins in his laver: to him be glory!

The Eighth Sunday of *Dinḥa*

Like a day that is filled and passes.

They will pass away, and you will remain.

The shadow of the Law has passed by means of the grace that has been revealed: for as the Hebrews were saved from slavery to the Egyptians by a lamb, thus were the Gentiles freed from ignorance by the epiphany of Christ; instead of the pillar of light which shone before the people, the Sun of Justice has risen, and, in place of Moses, Christ has come, and has saved and ransomed all our souls, that we may lift up praise to him, and thanksgiving every day.

The Lamb

The Old Testament is full of metaphors that God used to communicate his Divinity, love and plan to the people of Israel. Just as a child is introduced to difficult concepts through metaphor, God took Israel by the hand and, metaphor by metaphor, revealed his plan for their salvation. It all began with the lamb at Passover. The instructions for the lamb of this sacrifice were specific; "Your lamb shall be without blemish, a male a year old" (Exodus 12:5). Those who did not eat of the lamb and mark their doorposts with its blood were cut off from Israel. The only way to escape Egypt was by eating the lamb of Passover. For Israel, Egypt was the land of slavery and oppression. Though

57

there were many of them, they could not escape it alone. It took the power of God to free them from it.

God is much more forward with his people today. Through the Church, we now understand what the Israelites were only given to understand through metaphor. We do not kill a lamb without blemish in order to escape our slavery, we eat the true Lamb, the Lamb of God, Jesus. It is through this Lamb that we are rescued from our sinfulness and given a promise of eternal happiness, of a heavenly paradise. Unlike the Israelites who were given the fulfillment of God's promise on earth through the "Promised Land," we are given a much more eternal promise, that of Heaven and unity with God for eternity.

Freed From Ignorance

God is no longer hidden within a cloud that his glory may not smite the people of Israel. The light in our darkness is not a pillar by night. We see Jesus, unveiled and in glory. Our Sun of Justice is the Son of God Himself. In his revelation at the Baptism in the Jordan, we are given the revelation of the Trinity. Like children who are weaned from their mother's milk and given solid food, God no longer speaks to us in metaphor. He reveals himself fully in Jesus and through the Church. Where Moses was the mediator between God and Israel, we have the New Moses who leads us through the wilderness of our sinfulness and brings us to the Promised Land, the true paradise flowing with milk and honey:

The shadow of the Law has passed by means of the grace that has been revealed: for as the Hebrews were saved from slavery to the Egyptians by a lamb, thus were the Gentiles freed from ignorance by the epiphany of Christ; instead of the pillar of light which shone before the people, the Sun of Justice has risen, and, in place of Moses, Christ has come, and has saved and ransomed all our souls, that we may lift up praise to him, and thanksgiving every day.

Din_ha

The First Sunday of _Sawma_

O Lord, the God of my salvation.

We your people and the sheep of your flock.

O Lord, behold your Church, saved by your Cross, and your flock bought with your precious Blood offers a crown of thanksgiving in faith to you, O High Priest of justice who has exalted her by your abasement. And, like a glorious Bride, she rejoices and exults in you, O glorious Bridegroom. In the strength of the Truth, raise the walls of her salvation, and establish priests within her to be ambassadors of peace on behalf of her children.

Reversal

It is remarkable that the spiritual imagery for many of the hymns sung on this first Sunday of Lent has little or nothing to do with the act of fasting or even the idea of repentance. To a great extent, the discussion is one of Ecclesiology – the identity of the Church. It is as if the Lord, led by the Spirit into the wilderness, is accompanied by the whole Church: she is to follow him into the desert; she is to imitate his fasting and austerity; she, and all of us, her children, are to be with Christ in every step of his life.

Christ's unity with his Church takes on many aspects and is expressed, in Scripture and Tradition, using many symbols. The first section of our Basilica Hymn brings several together, before preparing for yet another:

O Lord, behold your Church, saved by your Cross, and your flock bought with your precious Blood offers a crown of thanksgiving in faith to you, O High Priest of justice who has exalted her by your abasement.

The Church is the body saved by his cross and the flock of the good Shepherd, but she is also the new Temple of the true High Priest, the one who offers not the blood of goats and bulls, but who came down from heaven to earth and offers his own precious Blood.

Where it had been the case that the Church (in a primordial state) was lowly and sinful, and the Son of God in the glory of heaven, one takes on the burden of the other: the Son becomes man, taking the form of a servant, and consequently, the Church becomes a queen.

The Narrow Door

This leads to the final image manifested by the Church: that of the Bride of the wondrous Bridegroom of heaven:

And, like a glorious Bride, she rejoices and exults in you, O glorious Bridegroom.

Though the Church is a Bride and a Queen, the doors to the bedchamber of this royal palace are not covered in gold or jewels, they are not the enormous slabs of fine mahogany we would expect adorning the inner sanctuary of the King of Kings. No, the door to this bedchamber is small and meek, and "those who enter it are few." In a very real sense, it is Christ who is himself the Door.

The Church, therefore, cannot enter this door if she is carrying with her the goods of this world, she cannot fit if she is bloated with the gluttony of greed. Material things and sensual pleasures must be left behind entirely if she is to enter, and this is the meaning of her fasting.

Offspring

The Church having entered, following after her Lord, the love between the Bridegroom and Bride is perfected, and the result is the fulfillment of the order given to Adam to "be fertile and multiply," as well as the promise given to Abraham regarding his many descendants: a multitude of children. Here the Church becomes a mother, and Christ completes his mission, becoming the perfect Image of the Father:

In the strength of the Truth, raise the walls of her salvation, and establish priests within her to be ambassadors of peace on behalf of her children.

The Second Sunday of *Ṣawma*

Come and glorify the Lord.

For his grace has increased upon us.

Come, let us all give thanks and glorify our good God, as much as we are able, for his benefits to our race: honor him for our establishment, from the beginning, in the Name of his honorable Image; and, when the enemy envied our honor and cast us out of our glory, he was revealed to us and spoke to us in his Son, who is the Inheritance and Progenitor of the world to come; in whose birth gathered us from the error of ignorance to the knowledge of his Divinity; who was baptized and gave us a true adoption; who fasted and gave encouragement to our weariness that we might overcome Satan; in whose death he conquered the tyrant; and who justified us, lifted us up and raised us with himself in glory.

A Fitting Introduction

Because of the descending nature of humanity after the fall, that is, because of the fact that our mind is so easily distracted from that which is right to that which it desires, the first focus of Lent was the relationship between the Lord and his Church rather than in some particular detail of our activities during this season. In the midst of our works of mercy and penance, it can be all too tempting to forget that the Lord and our union with him is the point of all that we do.

This week also, we refuse to be turned from our focus on Christ onto anything that we ourselves are doing. Even more so, we counter perhaps our own complaints with the aches and pains of the season, the blood and dust of the spiritual battle, with a heartfelt thanksgiving to God:

Come, let us all give thanks and glorify our good God, as much as we are able, for his benefits to our race...

During this second week of Lent, then, instead of the ordinary whining and murmuring of the human race, we lift up, in the name of Christ, thanksgiving to the God who gave us every good thing.

Context

The liturgical seasons are not isolated entities, but links in a chain that begins with the beginning of salvation history and ends with the Sanctification of the Crowned Church, with the work of Christ as the centerpiece and fulfillment of all grace. Therefore, when we recall, for example, the Ascension of the Lord to heaven, it is in a larger context: it comes after the season of the Resurrection and prepares the way for Pentecost and the season of the Apostles.

In the same way, the memorial of the fasting of the Lord in the desert is in a larger context. As in the Gospels, it is recalled directly after his baptism; that is, it comes after the season of

Epiphany. But ultimately the suffering of the Lord during these forty days is seen to reflect the light of his final suffering, death and resurrection. Our hymn therefore begins in the context of the very creation of the human race, and ends with the glorification of the Lord and the whole human race with him, placing his fasting and ours in their proper context:

> **...honor him for our establishment, from the beginning, in the Name of his honorable Image; and, when the enemy envied our honor and cast us out of our glory, he was revealed to us and spoke to us in his Son, who is the Inheritance and Progenitor of the world to come; in whose birth gathered us from the error of ignorance to the knowledge of his Divinity; who was baptized and gave us a true adoption; who fasted and gave encouragement to our weariness that we might overcome Satan; in whose death he conquered the tyrant; and who justified us, lifted us up and raised us with himself in glory.**

The Third Sunday of _Sawma_

Do not enter into judgment with your servant.
For you are righteous in your word and just in your judgments.
If you enter into judgment with your servant, O Lord God,
what excuse will I find? And where can I beg for forgiveness?
For I have rejected and broken all your laws, and have
become a dead man in the greatness of my sins. As from
Sheol, from the sea of sin draw me out, in your mercy: O
Christ the King, have mercy on me!

The Lord's Fasting and Ours

Among the reflections appropriate for Lent, the Great Fast, is that of sin. When Christ fasted for forty days in the desert and battled with Satan for our salvation, he could not reflect on his own sinfulness, because he is without sin. But while his fasting is an example to us, ours is of a different nature than his; he fasted in order to show us what to do, whereas we fast because we need to; he fasted in order to provide us with grace, whereas we fast because we are in such need of grace; he fasted to show the world his greatness and to destroy the power of Satan, whereas we fast to show ourselves our weakness and to beg for God's help in defeating Satan in our own lives.

Fasting as a Reminder

All of this implies how important it is to recall our sinfulness and our weakness, so that we may more earnestly beg for the mercy of God offered to us in the grace of Christ. Fasting, if it is done in accord with the wishes of the Church, is to result in humility. By it we are to know more vividly our need for God's aid. Indeed, fasting is among the finest weapons against spiritual pride.

When we begin to think of ourselves as pious and holy, we need only deprive ourselves of some simple desire to realize who we really are – how driven by our own wants and preoccupations, how distracted by silly desires, how grumpy when we are denied what we wish for; or, even worse, how quickly we can fall into arrogance and looking down on others when fasting is easy for us.

Without Excuse or Defense

The Basilica Hymn for the Third Sunday of *Ṣawma* is in precisely this spirit – it reflects an awareness of how far we fall without God's help, and how necessary grace is for us.

If you enter into judgment with your servant, O Lord God, what excuse will I find? And where can I beg for forgiveness?

Here the problem is presented under the aspect of judgment and forgiveness; the scene is set in this way: we are the subjects of the great King, and we have been called to present our case before him. But we cannot find any lawyer among our fellow subjects to defend us in court. Nor can we give any defense ourselves, or find an excuse for our actions, or even beg for forgiveness! The reason for this is that we "have rejected and broken all your laws," and as a result of this rebellion against the King who gave us life, you and I "have become a dead man in the greatness of my sins."

The imagery is deliberate and rich. The King of this World has given us so much more than any political leader – he has given us life itself. But along with this life he has asked that we follow his laws, as any Sovereign can reasonably do when he provides us with any good. Indeed, most of us are (rightly) so careful to follow the laws of the country which gives us freedom and prosperity. Otherwise, if we break its laws, the freedom and prosperity it gives us can be taken away. But what of the King who gives us life? What if we break his laws? Does he not have the right to take away the life he gave us for free? And so each one of us, no matter how great or how little our sins, are found in the same situation: having broken the laws of the King of life, we find ourselves spiritually dead "in the greatness of our sins."

The Merciful King

Then what are we to do? After sinning and sinning again, we have dug our own spiritual graves and have made our souls lifeless, rotting corpses, so much worse than the lepers who were healed by Christ, for our disease is deeper and even more difficult to cure. Sheol is the Semitic word for the "place of the dead," and the Basilica Hymn for this third week of Lent reminds us where we find ourselves by putting us there. But, after all of this, God has not given up on us and does not condemn us, for he has given the Kingdom to his Son, who has the power to save us even from spiritual death:

> **"As from Sheol, from the sea of sin draw me out, in your mercy: O Christ the King, have mercy on me!"**

As Christ pulled Peter up from drowning in the sea, and as it was only Christ who could have done so, we ask him to pull us out of the sea of sin in which we are drowning. "Mercy" is repeated for two reasons: first, because he does not owe us any help or salvation – that is, it is not something we deserve to ask for, and saving us is not something he owes us. It is a grace – that is, an undeserved gift. The second reason "mercy" is repeated is that it is an accurate description of this King to say he is "Merciful." Despite all of our sins, Christ our King has loved us enough to give his life for us and to save us from death.

The Fourth Sunday of *Ṣawma*

The heavens proclaim the glory of God.
Glorious and exalted are his works.
This world, in its construction, daily prepares and awakens
rational creatures to the wonder and glory of that wise
Creator. The wondrous variations, which oppose one
another, harmonize within it: fire, water, earth and vaporous
air. But that we may not be led astray and think that, because
of their diversity, they have many makers, he took and made,
of creation, one body in the forming of man, and in him made
known to us that he is the Lord of all.

Looking Around Us

One of the most natural sentiments of the Chaldean spiritual tradition is to gaze upon the world around us and stand in awe at the Creator. This might seem redundant to say – indeed, don't all Christians affirm that God created the universe, and don't all human beings find fascination in the world around them? Though that should ideally be the case, the complexity of human nature has proven otherwise. Many Christians, looking at the suffering and evil in this world, and looking forward to the perfect beatitude of heaven, can have a tendency to ignore or even look down upon this world, and to consider its beauty and order as flawed because it is not that of heaven. Even more so, theology aside, not every human being is able to see the marvel and wonder of nature. This may be because of any number of reasons: he may be embittered because of some particular evil that has found its way into his life; he may be consumed with some inner desire and unable to reflect on anything aside from it; he may be too busy even to pay attention! Indeed, though every spirit – every "rational creature" – was designed by the Creator to appreciate the beauty of the world, not all do. It takes a soul sensitive enough to notice and loving enough to make the effort to see the beauty of the natural world – and one humble enough to marvel at the "partialness" of the beauty of this world even in light of the perfect beauty of the world to come.

It is exactly this type of soul that is reflected in many of the writings of the Chaldean Church. In the Basilica Hymn of the Fourth Sunday of Lent, we are reminded of what a gift God gave us when he created the world for our sake – and this at an appropriate time. During Lent we turn away – not from "this world" in the sense of creation itself – but from the desires that are excessive and shallow and which keep us far from God. On the contrary, it is only when these misplaced emotions are put in check and mastered that we can truly appreciate the beauty and loveliness God has shown us even in this world.

The Movement of the World

Let us then turn to the reflection of God's light we find in the world he made: "**This world, in its construction, prepares and awakens rational creatures daily to the wonder and glory of that wise Creator.**" The author of our hymn is here fascinated mostly with the "construction" or "ordering" of the world, which he explains in more detail later. But we should notice here that the universe is the subject of two verbs – to "prepare" and to "awaken." Before we even consider the two verbs, we should realize a very important fact: the universe is not a passive "thing." It is not inactive or still or boring. In itself it is active and energetic and dynamic with power and movement. Moreover, this energy is a "**daily**" event; that is, although the activity of the universe it temporal (within time) and temporary (approaching an eventual end), it does not pause while it exists. It is not only during a sunset that the universe actively points our attention to its Creator, but at every moment.

Waking Up

The world "**prepares and awakens**" us to the "**wonder and glory**" of God. This implies that the first condition of our minds is unprepared and asleep, and evokes the image of the foolish virgins who did not bring oil with their lamps and then fell asleep before the coming of the Bridegroom in Matthew Chapter 25. While all ten virgins eventually were asleep, and only five were unprepared, creation supplies both preparation and wakefulness to our souls, that we may become daily aware of the wonder and glory of the Maker.

How does this happen? In what way does the world prepare us and awaken us to God's glory? The hymn continues: "**The wondrous variations, which oppose one another, harmonize within it: fire, water, earth and vaporous air**." The four elements of classical physics are shown in their opposition – earth is heavy and air is light, water is wet and fire is dry, etc. Therefore the very fact that they "**are harmonized**," or made to exist side-by-side, is marvelous enough. But the graciousness of God goes beyond this mere "preparation" of our minds through the harmony of opposite realities.

There is an even deeper reality, an even more shocking awareness that rouses us out of our spiritual sleep: "**And so that we may not be led astray to think that, because of their diversity, they have many makers, he took and made, of creation, one body in the forming of man, and in him made known to us that he is the Lord of all**." The Lord uses his creation to "**awaken**" us out of the spiritual sleep of idolatry (the worship of any creature) by reminding us that we have no excuse not to know him: we are created in his image! When any objective mind examines nature, it is naturally led to what is more complex, more beautiful, and better. This process ends when we reach the human being, the peak and culmination of all the created world, where all the elements combine in one gorgeous masterpiece.

Despite the pain we suffer, the Creator shows himself in something deeper. Despite the desires within us, the Creator offers us a greater beatitude. Despite our distractions, the Creator calls our attention to himself at every moment. We have no excuse if we do not know God, because his fingerprint is so "in our face" that we cannot miss it – it is in our very selves. We have no excuse if we fall asleep, because we are the alarm clock.

The Fifth Sunday of *Ṣawma*

For my life is spent in misery.

And my years in groaning.

The whole span of my life disperses and vanishes vainly in the confusion of the vanities of this world. And because I have not even desired, for a single hour, to prepare myself for tackling work in the spiritual vineyard, I do not expect to receive the wage prepared for the just. But, for the hidden wounds of my sins, I ask forgiveness from you, unworthy though I am. And so, before I stand before your frightful judgment-seat and am found guilty of my crimes by your just judgment, say the word, and I will be healed by your mercies: O Lover of mankind, glory to you!

Reflection on Life

It is possible to describe an average person's day thus: he wakes up in the morning to talk radio playing on his alarm clock, showers and prepares for the day, eats breakfast quickly or in the car, drives to work listening again to the radio, works vigorously all day with perhaps a short lunch, returns home the same way he got to work, has dinner, if he is lucky, with his family, sits in front of the television for a few hours to relax, then goes to sleep and starts over again the next day.

There is nothing painful or unpleasant about this life, but it is the saddest, most tragic life imaginable. Day after day, a life like this goes on without a single real thought. It wastes away without a moment of reflection. To live life like this is to never be aware that you are alive. To stop and think, to have silence and peace, is not the same as to "relax." In some sense it is the opposite. What we usually mean when we say "relax" is the negation of any thought. It means we do not want to think at all, and so we turn our mind to mindless things. Real silence is the opposite: we think about the most valuable, the most real things, and if we are honest in this endeavor, we eventually arrive at God. But this effort is impossible if every moment is spent either working or recovering from work. Time must be dedicated, and if we do not have such time, it means, perhaps, that we work too much, or that we relax too much.

The Painful Reflection

If thinking about life were completely pleasant, it would be much more common. But because there is an element of pain to it, it is easy to avoid. Indeed, it is quite possible for even prayer to take on a "business-like" nature and become a duty that is completed like mowing the lawn, just to get it done. This is especially sad, since prayer should be the most dramatic moment of the day, not just a list of needs we read off to God, or the blabbering of some memorized prayer.

But "dramatic" is not always "pleasant." Prayer, and the reflection that is both its prerequisite and its result, brings us nearer to the reality of truth, and sometimes the truth hurts. Especially if Christ is himself the Truth, as he himself said and as we profess, then encountering him can often be a challenge, since by his grace he is constantly calling us to deeper conversion.

In the end, when we begin a life of true prayer and reflection, we realize something very sad about ourselves:

The whole span of my life disperses and vanishes vainly in the confusion of the vanities of this world.

In a very real sense, we have wasted our lives – wasted them on the "vanities of this world" such as money (for which we "disperse" ourselves with work) and pleasure. And on the day we begin to look back and think for the first time, we realize that it was not a single day or week or year that was wasted, never to return, but the whole span of our lives. This is sad indeed, not only because of the waste, but because of what awaits us – the judgment of God, where he will ask us what we have done with our time and our talents.

Working in the Vineyard

In Matthew chapter 20, the Lord describes the kingdom of heaven as a vineyard with workers who were hired at various hours of the day: dawn, morning, noon, afternoon and evening.

The last workers hired worked for only an hour, and received the same wage as those who worked the entire day. The generosity of the landowner is not unjust: it was not by any fault of their own that the final workers worked only an hour. Indeed, the reason they did not work all day is not by choice but because no one hired them.

But what about us? We have neglected to work for God by choice, and so what could our payment be?

And because I have not even desired, for a single hour, to prepare myself for tackling work in the spiritual vineyard, I do not expect to receive the wage prepared for the just.

The language in this phrase is complex even to the point of being cumbersome, and it must be. It is not simply that we have not "worked," like those in the parable who wanted to but could not. Nor have we merely neglected to make ourselves ready or "prepare" ourselves. We have not even desired to prepare ourselves to work. That being the case, it is our own fault that we have not worked in the vineyard, and we have no reason to expect a wage from our Lord.

Not a Worker but a Sick Man

The imagery of our hymn then changes from the robust, healthy worker of Christ's parable to the sickly leper or servant of reality, described by the Gospel writers. No longer are we considering the ideal believers of Christ's words, the kingdom of heaven described by our Lord; now we consider this world and ourselves as a part of it. But it was precisely into this world that our Lord was born, and in this world that he ministered, healing the sick of soul and body. It is into our world that he places himself, and in our lives where he still dwells today.

But, for the hidden wounds of my sins, I ask forgiveness from you, unworthy though I am.

We have the confidence, even the daring, to ask something we do not deserve through the grace of Christ, who reconciled us to God through his Blood. In the end, it is upon his grace that we base our hope, and upon his mercy that we dare to ask for healing and forgiveness:

And so, before I stand before your frightful judgment-seat and am found guilty of my crimes by your just judgment, say the word, and I will be healed by your mercies: O Lover of mankind, glory to you.

The Sixth Sunday of *Ṣawma*

My sores have rotted and putrefied.

From where will come my help?

"Who is the doctor who can cleanse my hidden wounds? O, will he be able to heal and to cure them? O who will be able to deliver me from the fire?" thus cried the adulteress. "I will unravel the tangles of sin, and draw near to the Lord and Savior." For indeed, he did not cast the tax-collector away from him, and with his speech, he converted the Samaritan woman. With his word, he gave life to the Canaanite woman, and to the hemorrhaging woman he gave healing with the hem of his cloak. With his merciful word, he freed the adulteress from her sins, and summoned her to the book of life with the holy women. Along with them, my soul says at all times: Blessed is the Messiah our Savior!

The Divine Physician

There are many occasions in this world to be surprised, and many times when we meet with something completely unexpected. We have seen, in the past few weeks, that we can find many wonderful, positive things in the world around us that God created. His own glory is shown in the things he has made. But the reality of surprise has a dark side as well. While we marvel at the beauty of God and his works, we are shocked at the ugliness of human sin.

81

Being the selfish beings we are, it is easier for us to concentrate on the faults of others and to be bothered by them. To look at the harm that someone else has caused and be disgusted is a common enough experience. But what about when we look within? What about when we see our own faults, our own awful choices? How disgusting can we make ourselves with sin! How ugly do we paint our souls! The English exclamation "sick!" is doubly appropriate here: it means both "disgusting" and "diseased," and that is exactly what we are.

"Who is the doctor who can cleanse my hidden wounds? O, will he be able to heal and to cure them?" The character of the adulterous woman of the Gospels is brought to the forefront in the Basilica Hymn of the Sixth Sunday of Lent as a symbol for each of our souls. She speaks, on our behalf, of spiritual wounds, self-inflicted and festering with rottenness. Medically, she knows that, as with a physical wound, even her spiritual wounds need cleaning, but she is stuck in a sad state: what doctor can tend to an invisible wound? How can any human being even see the dirt stuck inside to begin to clean it? And this is only the first stage of healing! Even after a wound is cleaned, it requires binding up and care, and time to heal.

Without a doctor who can see the soul itself, the wounds we have only continue to fester and rot, and become worse and worse over time, burning us with the pain of regret and guilt, and pulling us to sin again and again, making us wound ourselves more and more deeply. "**'O who will be able to deliver me from the fire?' thus cried the adulteress."**

The Messiah names himself the doctor of souls when he is confronted by the Pharisees in Matthew chapter 9. "Those who are well do not need a physician, but the sick do." Christ is everything we need, filling our every void and fulfilling our deepest hopes, and so he is also the healer, the doctor, of our spiritual wounds, the one whom the adulteress sought, the one whom we seek.

Hope

The image of the adulteress is quite widespread in the Scriptures. In the Old Testament, the people of Israel are compared to an adulterous wife when they sin against the Lord, and their idolatry is compared to adultery. But the power of this image is most meaningful when we realize God's reaction: he does not reject the unfaithful bride, but forgives her again and again, patiently teaching her and bringing her back to himself.

It is this hope that the adulteress has: "I will unravel the tangles of sin, and draw near to the Lord and Savior." The narrator of the hymn then takes up his own voice, explaining the affirmation of the adulteress, showing why she has a solid basis for this hope, and why we do as well:

For indeed, he did not cast the tax-collector away from him, and with his speech, he converted the Samaritan woman. With his word, he gave life to the Canaanite woman, and to the hemorrhaging woman he gave healing with the hem of his cloak. With his merciful word, he freed the adulteress from her sins, and summoned her to the book of life with the holy women.

We can trust that Jesus will heal us when we turn to him, because he has proven his mercy to so many.

We no longer need to sit and pick at our wounds, feeling the pangs of remorse and hurting our souls more and more with sin. We have a doctor who can see all, who can read our hearts and touch them with his grace. It is significant that all but one of the people healed by Christ mentioned in our hymn is a woman, because the word "soul" (*nawsha*) in Aramaic is a feminine noun, and so the individual soul can be represented by all of the healings mentioned. Thus the hymn ends: **Along with them, my soul says at all times: Blessed is the Messiah our Savior!**

Doctors and Disciples

The same Christ who walked before that adulteress and forgave her sins, healing her hidden wounds is still with us, except now he is invisible and is approached by faith. Seeing him work through his Holy Spirit in the Church requires belief in his healing power stretching from heaven to earth. And as he worked in the flesh as he walked in Jerusalem, so he works through his disciples today, "in Spirit and in truth."

"'As the Father has sent me, so I send you.' And when he had said this, he breathed on them and said to them, 'Receive the Holy Spirit. Whose sins you forgive are forgiven them, and whose sins you retain are retained.'" (John 20:22-23). In his Name, the apostles forgave sins and in his Name do their successors do the same. One of the earliest pieces of evidence in the whole universal Church of individual "Confession," as we call it today, is found in our own Chaldean liturgy, and it uses the same image we have been discussing, that of the Divine Doctor:

> Our Lord has given the medicine of repentance
> to the skilled physicians who are the priests of the Church.
> So let anyone whom satan has struck
> with the diseases of wickedness
> come and show his wounds to the disciples of the Wise Physician,
> and they will heal him with spiritual medicine.

Hosanna Sunday

Remember your Church, which you acquired from the beginning.
Like a glorious Bridegroom; like an adorned bride.

O Lord, behold your Church, saved by your Cross, and your flock bought with your precious Blood, offers a crown of thanksgiving in faith to you, O High Priest of justice who has exalted her by your abasement. And, like a glorious Bride, she rejoices and exults in you, O glorious Bridegroom. In the strength of the Truth, raise the walls of her salvation, and establish priests within her, to be ambassadors of peace on behalf of her children.

Glory to the Father, and to the Son, and to the Holy Spirit.

When you were entering Jerusalem, the holy city, O Christ, God and our King, to fulfill all that had been written, young people and children saw you with the enlightened eye of faith and were amazed by you, as they picked up branches and went out to meet you. They threw garments and cloaks on your path, and all cried out the unending praise of the cherubim, as they said: "Hosanna in the highest! Blessed are you who has eternally abounding mercies!" O Lord of all, have mercy on us!

Seeing Again, for the First Time

The beginning and end of Lent share the same Basilica Hymn, which ties the two together and gives the whole season meaning. It may seem like a repetition or a redundancy to pray the same hymn twice in one season (and once again, in fact, in the season called the Crowning of the Church), but it is not so. On the contrary, reading the same words when there has been a change in the heart reveals new meaning. This is why the Holy Scriptures are ever new, always challenging the mind of mankind to greater understanding, though they are the same words that have been read for so many centuries. The very young can read the Bible, and understand it on their own level, and the old can read the same words they have been reading for decades, and find something new in them. The old can understand this better, perhaps: to revisit the same place years later is not the same as being there for the first time; it has an entirely new meaning, not because the place has changed, but because the person has.

Thus we revisit the same hymn we sang at the beginning of Lent. How have we changed during this season? If we read it with the same eyes, then we have failed and have rejected the graces being poured out during these weeks. If we have accepted Christ's graces, then we are closer to him, and see with newer eyes, eyes more like his. Let us look:

O Lord, behold your Church, saved by your Cross, and your flock bought with your precious Blood, offers a

crown of thanksgiving in faith to you, O High Priest of justice who has exalted her by your abasement. And, like a glorious Bride, she rejoices and exults in you, O glorious Bridegroom. In the strength of the Truth, raise the walls of her salvation, and establish priests within her, to be ambassadors of peace on behalf of her children.

Mixed Metaphors

The hymn is a mixture of several metaphors. In fact, by modern standards, it is confused and excessive; it is bad poetry. But it is not for modern standards, especially secular ones, to judge ancient spiritual hymns. Secular poetry attempts, with varying levels of success, to describe a reality within the human heart, and to do so expressively. The hymns of the Church of the East have a different goal entirely: they attempt to describe a heavenly reality – a reality beyond humanity completely – by using not merely human language, but the language contained in the Holy Scriptures, which is a mingling of human and divine expression. Thus her hymns cannot always have a single metaphor, such as "Christ the Divine Doctor" or "Christ the Good Shepherd." Sometimes the reality is too far beyond one idea to use one analogy.

The beginning of the Gospel of John uses a similar mixture of images: Word, Life, Light, Son, Truth, etc., all within a few verses. The images used in our hymn are as follows:

1. the Church as saved by the Cross

2. the Church as the flock of the good Shepherd

3. the Church as bought or purchased by Christ's blood

4. the Church as responding to Christ with the "crown of thanksgiving"

5. Christ as the High Priest

6. the Church as the Bride of Christ

7. the Church as a spiritual building with "walls of salvation"

8. the Church as a mother pleading for her children

To see these images at the beginning of Lent is to see them in anticipation – the Church realizes that her King is coming, and so she gets ready to present herself to him by her fasting, prayer, penance and almsgiving. But not now; now she sees the images reflecting her King who has come at last.

Palm Sunday

Children's stories can be among the most deeply rooted in human nature and self-understanding. The ogre or monster therein is more than a symbol; he is the personification of what we fear. The kingdom of the prince is neither a physical place nor the representation of any political ideal; it is perfection. The queen is not the person of the ruler, but neither is the king the idea of power. Every element in such legends is more basic than we imagine, and more meaningful.

Even more so is this the case with Biblical images. Their reality is not only beneath our consciousness, it is beyond our imagination. This is certainly the case with the image of the Church as the Bride of Christ, in some ways the most predominant image in all of Scripture. The basic concept is simple: the unity of God and humanity as compared to the union between a husband and his wife. But such a simple concept soars to sublime heights when the image is applied, and the more we draw from it, the more we realize it is inexhaustible. The season of the "Sanctification of the Church" is the proper place to discuss the gifts of the Bridegroom to his Bride, the dowry given to her, the wedding dress of Light, etc. Today, on Palm Sunday, we reflect on one particular moment in the relationship between Christ and the Church. Today we watch the King return for his Queen – as basic and primordial an image as any other in classical literature or in children's stories.

Christ the King returns to Jerusalem, which, fulfilling the prophecies of the Old Testament, comes out to meet him as his earthly Bride. The city itself becomes a representative, a precursor, of the Church to come, and as the Queen she welcomes her King with jubilation.

Historicity

There are times when words are too weak to express what we mean, when explanations become insulting because they fall so short. This week and its events are beyond words, beyond explanation. During such times when the most basic elements of the human heart are addressed, when the deepest part of his psyche is pierced, as with a needle, only actions are expressive enough.

No word is the right word when, for example, two friends part, never to see each other again. Not only is a glance enough, but to add to it would be ridiculous, almost shameful. No conversation could express the depth of emotion and reality occurring at that moment. Such is Holy Week. Words and explanations are so beyond us that we move to a different mode of communication: that of historical representation. Beginning on Palm Sunday, the Chaldean Church remembers history literally and chronologically. She lives every day with her Lord; she comes out to meet him as he enters Jerusalem, and does not part from his side until he is raised from the tomb. This is why we carry branches at Mass on Sunday, and process into the Church; this is why we begin saying "hosanna" again for the first time since before Lent began: we are re-living history. Thus, the second half of the hymn for Palm Sunday is not a reflection, a theological statement, or even a poetic image. It is simply the statement of a historical fact, and for this week, that is more than enough:

When you were entering Jerusalem, the holy city, O Christ, God and our King, to fulfill all that had been written, young people and children saw you with the enlightened eye of faith and were amazed by you, as they picked up branches and went out to meet you. They threw garments and cloaks on your path, and all cried out the unending praise of the cherubim, as they said: "Hosanna in the highest! Blessed are you who has eternally abounding mercies!" O Lord of all, have mercy on us!

Holy Saturday

The whole earth trembled and shook.

The foundations of the earth trembled.

When you hung on the cross, O Christ our Lord,

The creation saw you naked and the whole world shook;

The lamp of the sun turned into dark,

And the temple tore its veil,

And the dead rose up from their graves,

Giving praise to you, Resurrecting Lord!

The dead came forth from their tombs.

In our Lord's passion was true suffering,

Awe and wonder seized the angels and the sons of men:

The dead who were buried left their tombs,

Singing "glory to the Son,

Who came down and was crucified,

Who cried with his voice, Shaking heaven and earth!"

Wake, O Adam from of old:

See the Sole-Begotten Son,

Suffering like a sinful one

At the hands of sinful men!

Wake, O cheated Abel just,

Murdered by brother unjust,

see the Savior of the world

dies for the life of the world!

Wake, O innocent Noah,

God's replacement for the world,

see the Son of God Most High,

who hangs upon wood today!

Wake, O sons of blessings both,

Shem and honorable Japheth,

who covered the nakedness

of their father as he slept:

Come and see the sun above,

And the moon, the lamp of night,

Turn themselves to dark and gloom,

Lest their Lord be seen disgraced!

Wake, high priest Melchezidech,

who offered his sacrifice:

come today and see the Son

who has offered bread and wine!

Wake, O Father Abraham,

see the Son revealed to you:

he hangs upon wood today,

as did the ram shown to you.

Wake, O blessed Isaac, saved

by a ram caught in a tree,

see that true great mystery

fulfilled by your Lord today!

Wake, O Joseph, righteous one,

by his brethren spat upon,

see the Savior Jesus Christ

spit upon now by their sons!

Wake, O Moses, prophet great,

see the Lord of prophecy,

suff'ring for the prophets' sons,

as foretold by prophecy!

Wake, heroic Joshua,

who stopped the sun and the moon:

see, they wear darkness and gloom,

due to the death of the Son!

Wake, O Psalmist, David King,

come out of the grave today;

take up harp and lyre again,

and, preaching, sing us a Psalm:

"They divided his clothing,

placed their bets upon his robe,

and were like wild dogs around

the Lion who answered not."

Wake, arise, King Solomon,

sea of knowledge and wisdom,

see the Lord of all wisdom

who is mocked by ignorance!

Wake, O glorious Isaiah,

look and see the Christ and King;

bearing death, a Sacrifice,

without his mouth opening!

Wake, O Jonah, who for three days

was like a man dead in grave,

and who showed us, his own way,

resurrection in three days!

Wake, O Jeremiah, priest,

who was thrown into the mud,

see your Lord today asleep,

for whom a tomb is a bed!

Wake, O Zechariah blest,

and his son John the Baptist,

see today your Lord become

sacrifice and offering!

Wake, arise, O Patriarchs,

who died in hope of new life,

and see, upon Golgotha,

the Lord of all that is made!

Wake, arise, all you deceased,

see the dead with the living,

who preach to all the living,

the Lord of dead and living!

Wake, deceased from ages past,

see the Son who is of old,

who took your form in his love,

in whom Scripture is fulfilled!

Wake, you who are dead in sin,

see the Son who knows not sin,

who dies with the slaves of sin,

that he may kill death and sin!

Wake, deceased, the wonder see:

on the cross, the first-born Son,

by whose death has rent the earth

by whose death has death destroyed!

Conqueror, **Abandoned One,**

Judged by servants by his choice:

let us conquer all our sins

in your mercies which made us!

Blest **your death, and glorious**

is your rising from the dead;

pity us; forgive our sins,

by your grace which is our hope!

To you, **with your Father be**

adoration and glory,

and to the Spirit Holy,

forever, from age to age.

An Uncommon Commentary

The tradition of the Catholic Church is the richest spiritual heritage in history, and it provides, by the grace of Christ, the strongest link to Christ himself, the one Savior and Mediator between us and the Father. But the richness of the One Catholic Church is not monotone; it is nuanced and varied, and spread out over the various branches of the one Church – the traditions and "particular churches" which form it together, each contributing its part.

The contribution of the Chaldean Church to the entirety of the Catholic Faith is second to none, and the Basilica Hymn of

Holy Saturday, "The Saturday of Light," is a contribution that no other particular church has accomplished. It is a commentary on a verse of the Bible that is avoided by most commentators, both because it is difficult to explain as a historical circumstance and because even its spiritual significance is obscure. The verse is Matthew 27:50-53: "And Jesus cried again with a loud voice and yielded up his spirit. And behold, the curtain of the temple was torn in two, from top to bottom; and the earth shook, and the rocks were split; the tombs also were opened, and many bodies of the saints who had fallen asleep were raised, and coming out of the tombs after his resurrection they went into the holy city and appeared to many."

No other church has had the courage to interpret with such depth such an odd passage, claiming that many of the dead were raised and came out of their graves when Christ died on the Cross. What could the significance of this event be for the souls of the faithful who read the Gospel?

Sleep No More

Every event in history had led up to the passion, death and resurrection of Christ. This was the climax of everything that had happened before, which had been prefigured and prophesied by the entire Old Testament. Therefore, the Chaldean Church made an attempt to tie all of history together into this one moment, by "waking up" all the "sleeping" prophets who had awaited the Messiah, and to point out to them the fulfillment of all of their hopes. Beginning with Adam and ending with Zechariah and John the Baptist, one by one, the most significant of the prophets are "awakened" and shown the dead Messiah hanging upon the Cross.

Resurrection Sunday

Have mercy on me, God, in your kindness

Turn to me and have mercy on me

Like a dry and wearied land that needs water

Around the tomb, Mary cried "Have pity on me!" for she was remembering you who made her a dwelling of your love, instead of a dwelling of demons. She had bought spices to perfume your honorable body, in which the scent of our mortal race was perfumed. "By your Resurrection, O Good Lord of the deceased, I beg you, O Tree of Live, who raised Adam who transgressed, O Fruit that our race did not want to taste, my Savior, may the dew of your mercies sprinkle me!"

Glory to the Father and to the Son and to the Holy Spirit

After your glorious Resurrection, an evil and deceitful people made centurions stand to guard your tomb. Woe to that unbelieving people! If they killed and buried, why were they standing guard? And if they were terrified of you, how did they dare crucify you? Indeed, your Resurrection on the third day has shamed your crucifiers, and gladdened your Church. Glory to you!

The First Witness

In all four accounts of the Gospel, the first person mentioned as a witness to the event of the Resurrection of Christ, the foundation of our Christian faith, is Mary Magdalene. There were other women, but she is the most consistently named and always the first.

As in other powerful moments during Holy Week, so at this moment of the Resurrection the Church of the East enters into the heart of one of the personalities of the Gospel and expresses herself through her. A few days earlier, we joined Peter at the precise moment when he had denied Christ the third time and had broken down and wept. The precise moment we join Mary Magdalene is also of high significance: it is not when she first saw the tomb empty when she was with the other women, but rather after she had run back to tell the apostles, returned to the tomb with them, waited until Peter and John had left, and was sitting there alone, in the coolness of the early morning. This, the quietest moment of the story, is the most marvelous and the one during which our hymn takes place.

The tenderness of Mary Magdalene's sentiment is well expressed, and the entry into her psyche and her memory is powerful:

Around the tomb, Mary cried "Have pity on me!" for she was remembering you who made her a dwelling of your love, instead of a dwelling of demons.

The Spices

In the stillness around her, Mary recalled the goodness of the Lord who had saved her from demonic possession, one of the few actual facts recorded about Mary Magdalene in the Gospels. This Jesus who had changed her life completely, who had taken her from misery and given her healing of body and soul, the one whom she followed thereafter, had been killed a few days before:

She had bought spices to perfume your honorable body, in which the scent of our mortal race was perfumed.

Our author begins to move from historic and psychological analysis to a more poetic endeavor, comparing the spices Mary brought to disguise the scent of what she thought would be a decaying body to the graces poured out by the death of Christ. What is brought out by this image is the contrast between the human race in sin and the Body of Christ: we are the ones who are dead and rotting, and in need of the perfume of grace that comes from the Body of Christ, not the other way around.

The Gardener

The hymn ends in a remarkable display of delicacy. We know from the Gospel accounts that Mary then saw Christ himself, but confused him for a gardener. This image is utilized poetically by our author, while the actual event of the meeting is not referred to at all. It is almost as if it is too tender a moment to be described. Mary Magdalene prays silently:

"By your Resurrection, O Good Lord of the deceased, I beg you, O Tree of Live, who raised Adam who transgressed, O Fruit that our race did not want to taste, my Savior, may the dew of your mercies sprinkle me!"

The image of the gardener brings everything together – not simply the theological richness of the scene, but the very history of salvation. Adam sinned by tasting from the wrong tree, the tree of knowledge of good and evil. The other tree, the tree of life, was left aside by Adam and, after his sin, guarded by an angel. The vegetation of the garden of Eden is brought to the forefront by our hymn, and Christ himself is named both the Tree of Life and the Fruit of Immortality that is eaten and which destroys death. Mary ends her prayer by a final natural image: because we are unworthy to approach the Tree of Life, we must be purified first by the dew of Christ's mercies – dew, the water found on plants in the early morning, which both cleanses and nourishes.

Solidity

Because our faith is not simply spiritualism, belief in some mystical philosophy, but is Incarnate, that is, tied to historical events and especially to a historical personage, Jesus Christ, the fact of the Resurrection is of highest importance. In fact, in 1 Corinthians, St. Paul states that if Christ is not risen, then our faith is in vain. Christianity, then, is not like Buddhism or Platonism or Communism: it is not simply a set of ideas claiming to make sense of the world. It is more than that, and its foundation is not any floating, nebulous idea. Its foundation is Christ himself, and his Resurrection; its foundation is the empty tomb, seen first by Mary Magdalene and witnessed by the disciples.

In light of this, the second segment of the Basilica Hymn of Easter, the greatest feast of the liturgical year, is an argument for the Resurrection. It is as if we are the jury looking at the evidence of what truly happened on that day, and the author is the lawyer defending the Christian faith:

After your glorious Resurrection, an evil and deceitful people made centurions stand to guard your tomb. Woe to that unbelieving people! If they killed and buried, why were they standing guard? And if they were terrified of you, how did they dare crucify you? Indeed, your Resurrection on the third day has shamed your crucifiers, and gladdened your Church. Glory to you!

Though it happened to be the priests and elders of the Jewish people at the time of Christ who conspired to crucify him and who asked for Roman guards to be placed at the tomb, it is to any who do not believe that our author gives "woe." That is, the point is not a nationality but a lack of faith.

The argument itself is based on the self-contradicting actions of the nonbelievers: having the audacity to crucify the Messiah, they fear his disciples may steal his body. One the one hand they are anxious enough to call on the help of the Roman army, on the other hand they are bold enough to put a man to death. But the end, the presence of the Roman soldiers became another piece of evidence for the Resurrection, for it makes it much more difficult to believe that the disciples could steal the body:

Indeed, your Resurrection on the third day has shamed your crucifiers, and gladdened your Church. Glory to you!

The Week of Weeks

The earth was shaken and trembled.

The foundations of the mountains trembled and were shaken.

In the hour that the wood of your cross was fastened, you shook the foundations of death, O Lord. And those whom Sheol had swallowed in their sins, it released while trembling – your command quickened them, O Lord. Because of this, we also glorify you, O Christ the King:

Have mercy on us!

Come, let us bless and adore him.

His holy name forever and ever.

We adore the Memorial of your honorable Passion, O Savior, and also your Cross, which prepared a joyful feast for us. In it, we all accept the forgiveness of debts and sins, and new life apart from Sheol dawns for us, as well as the reproof of the Jews, the boast of your faithful Church, and the glory of your victorious unending power!

Where can I go from your Spirit?

And where can I hide from you?

In the hour when, in the midst of silence, the trumpet of your coming sounds in great fearfulness, and the awesome legions of the angels fly down in turbulence, and when all men arise from the graves, trembling in their inquisition, the heavenly hosts will shake from the vehemence of the judgment of the earthly, when the Cherubim carrying you extol you, O Just

107

Judge, indeed, in that fearful judgment when the actions of each man are repaid, have mercy on me, O Lover of mankind!

I will exult you, O Lord my King.
He lifts me up from the doors of death.
Your death, Lord Jesus, became the beginning of new life for us. And through baptism into you, we receive the token of life to come, which is your resurrection from among the dead. And so, in feasting rejoicings, we glorify your Name, O Lord, because you abolished error and took away the sin of the world. And the one on whose head was placed the decree of Adam's condemnation, you returned to life everlasting.

I will bless the Lord at all times.
And blessed be his honored name forever.
Blessed is the hidden power that dwells in the bones of the martyrs: for they are situated in their graves, and they chase demons out of the world. Through their teaching, they abolished the error of idolaters, and they quietly visit creation, and teach it to worship you, who alone are the Lord.
Glory to the Father and to the Son and to the Holy Spirit.
Glory to you, O good and kind Lord, in whose power your true ones were victorious, and in whose aid scorned the threats of their persecutors, and destroyed the power of the haughty enemy. For he saw that the martyrs did not fall away from their true foundation.

The First Day of the Week

The new Sabbath, the new Day of the Lord, is Sunday, the first day of the week. The old Sabbath, Saturday, has been superseded, though after the act of creation "God blessed the seventh day and made it holy, because on it he rested from all the work he had done in creation." (Genesis 2:3) The reason is that the Lord is now more than the Creator; he is the Redeemer, the Savior, in actuality as opposed to anticipation. Before Christ, the People of God awaited his salvation; we need wait no longer. Our salvation has arrived, and the day the Lord rested from all the work he had done in Salvation is Sunday, the day he rose from the dead. That this day became the replacement for the Sabbath of the Jews is witnessed in the Acts of the Apostles 20:7, which mentions that Sunday was the day the disciples "gathered to break bread."

This week, the week after Easter, has a Basilica Hymn for every day, not only for Sunday and Feast Days, which is usually the case for Basilica Hymns. This is our Liturgy telling us that the Feast of the Resurrection of our Lord is not an event whose joy can be exhausted in a single day or two – every day of this week is a feast, is a Sunday, is an entire week in itself – "The Week of Weeks."

109

Monday

In the hour that the wood of your cross was fastened, you shook the foundations of death, O Lord. And those whom Sheol had swallowed in their sins, it released while trembling – your command quickened them, O Lord. Because of this, we also glorify you, O Christ the King: Have mercy on us!

Historical remembrance and the depth of sentiment found simply in the events themselves was the focus of all of Holy Week, but now, the events having been recalled to the fullest degree by our re-presentation of them, we begin to look back and reflect, gazing a second and third time upon what has transpired in the days past. Monday, we strike to the root of the problem – death itself, and Sheol (the place of the dead) as our main enemy. The death of Christ on the cross defeated our oldest enemy, and through his resurrection he becomes the new King before whom even death and Sheol shake and tremble in fear and obedience.

Tuesday

We adore the Memorial of your honorable Passion, O Savior, and also your Cross, which prepared a joyful feast for us. In it, we all accept the forgiveness of debts and sins, and new life apart from Sheol dawns for us, as well as the reproof of the Jews, the boast of your faithful Church, and the glory of your victorious unending power!

Because no photograph or journal could encapsulate the depth of the salvific act of the Messiah in his death, burial and resurrection, and indeed no human form of remembrance at all is up to the task, Christ himself had to give us the most powerful reminder of all: the Holy Eucharist. Such is its memorial power that it brings us – sacramentally and completely – back to the events themselves, and gives us access to their power: forgiveness of sins and new life.

Wednesday

In the hour when, in the midst of silence, the trumpet of your coming sounds in great fearfulness, and the awesome legions of the angels fly down in turbulence, and when all men arise from the graves, trembling in their inquisition, the heavenly hosts will shake from the vehemence of the judgment of the earthly, when the Cherubim carrying you extol you, O Just Judge, indeed, in that fearful judgment when the actions of each man are repaid, have mercy on me, O Lover of mankind!

From recalling the past, we turn to thinking about the future. The beginning of salvation points to the end of time, when Christ will come with his angels and judge all the people of the earth. He comes forth, not as a child in a manger or as a teacher on a mountain or as a sacrifice on a cross, but as a Judge of perfect Justice. With that in mind, we tremble and ask for mercy from the One who not only judges us justly, but loves us mercifully.

Thursday

Your death, O Lord Jesus, became the beginning of new life for us. And through baptism into you, we receive the token of life to come, which is your resurrection from among the dead. And so, in feasting rejoicings, we glorify your Name, O Lord, because you abolished error and took away the sin of the world. And the one on whose head was placed the decree of Adam's condemnation, you returned to life everlasting.

The Church celebrates the redemption of Christ in all actuality, not simply as a memory, because his redemption is actual and present to us, not hidden in the past. His death was the beginning of new life, a life which is continually expressed through baptism, in which we are cleansed by sacramentally dying to sin and rising with Christ, and through the feasts of the Church, in which we continually live in communion with the Messiah.

Friday of the Confessors

Blessed is the hidden power that dwells in the bones of the martyrs: for they are situated in their graves, and they chase demons out of the world. Through their teaching, they abolished the error of idolaters, and they quietly visit creation, and teach it to worship you, who alone are the Lord.

Glory to you, O good and kind Lord, in whose power your true ones were victorious, and in whose aid scorned the threats of their persecutors, and destroyed the power of the haughty enemy – for he saw that the martyrs did not fall away from their true foundation.

By "Confessors" we mean those witnesses to the resurrection of Christ who gave their lives in telling this truth, on whose testimony our faith relies, since we were not there in Jerusalem or Galilee to see Christ risen ourselves. "Blessed are they who believe but do not see," is a blessing that is available to us through their testimony. Indeed, this fact alone is enough to confound a nonbeliever: if Christ is not risen from the dead in truth, how can you explain the claims of these witnesses who gave up their lives saying he did?

Saturday

You have abolished and loosened, through your holy cross, O Christ the King, all the error of idols, and you have exalted and honored all those who believe in you. For lo, the splendid Service of your hidden and holy Mysteries is extolled like a bride in honoring the martyrs who were killed for your sake. The priests who sing, and we also who glorify you, say: O Lord, may the true faith be guarded until eternity!

Past, present and future mingle in this final hymn of the Week of Weeks; past tense in "abolished and loosened," referring to Christ's work accomplished on the cross; present in the Service of Mass, occurring every day in the Church; future in our song of supplication, asking for the faith to be guarded until the end of time. Thus, all of time, all of history, is summarized in the Redemption of Christ.

The Second Sunday
of the Resurrection
"New Sunday"

I will exult you, O Lord, my King.
It was at the head of the building.

Your resurrection, O Savior, adorned our race with heavenly gifts: it gave us, immediately, a true new life in the spiritual birth of baptism, in which we are baptized in the model of your Death and Resurrection; it also established, for us, teachers and priests in the churches, through whose agency we are brought near to the glorious Mysteries of the knowledge of your Divinity. O Lover of mankind, glory to you!

Results of the Resurrection

What we mean when we say an event is "major" is that its consequences are far-reaching. World wars are "major" events; floods, earthquakes and other natural catastrophes as well. This is because they affect the world in a significant way and for a significant time after their occurrence. That is, they do not just "happen" and go away. Their residue clings to the world, and the mark they leave behind remains to remind us of them.

This is not only the case with negative events, but with positive ones as well. The ordination of a priest is a single event, as is the wedding of two people. But these momentary events change people's lives for decades after their occurrence; not simply the people in question (the priest or the new husband and wife), but others as well.

What, then, is the far-reaching significance of the event of the Resurrection of Christ? If indeed it is the most important, dramatic, "major" event in the history of humanity, which we indeed claim, its consequences must be proportionately major. The Basilica Hymn for the Second Sunday of Easter, called "New Sunday" or, as I have translated it above, "The New Day," mentions some of the results of this striking moment:

Your resurrection, O Savior, adorned our race with heavenly gifts: it gave us, immediately, a true new life in the spiritual birth of baptism, in which we are baptized in the model of your Death and Resurrection; it also established, for us, teachers and priests in the churches, through whose agency we are brought near to the glorious Mysteries of the knowledge of your Divinity. O Lover of mankind, glory to you!

116

The Immediate Earthquake

The first of the "heavenly gifts" given to us by the resurrection of Christ that is named in our hymn is the sacrament of baptism. The connection between the baptism of the Church and the resurrection of Christ is well explained by St. Paul: "Are you unaware that we who were baptized into Christ Jesus were baptized into his death? We were indeed buried with him through baptism into death, so that, just as Christ was raised from the dead by the glory of the Father, we too might live in newness of life." (Romans 6:2-4)

Thus, the power of the resurrection over death itself, our oldest enemy, is poured out upon us at our baptism, which is, in the language of our hymn "in the model of" Christ's death and resurrection. That is, in the "old days," in fact even within recent memory in the Chaldean Church, the person to be baptized was dipped entirely under the water, imitating Christ's descent into the grave and Sheol, and then came up out of the water, imitating Christ's resurrection and victory over the grave. What an enormous effect! What an earthquake! Death is defeated and destroyed through this sacrament which is a direct result of the resurrection.

The Tremors Heard Till Today

In addition to baptism, the first and immediate successor of the resurrection, the hymn we examine this week names another effect: "it also established teachers and priests for us in the churches, through whose agency we are brought near to the glorious Mysteries of the knowledge of your Divinity." Teachers and priests, which are still with us today along with baptism, are those who unite us to the knowledge of God which allows us to grow in friendship with him through grace.

Another fitting result of such a marvelous event: we earthly beings, sinners made from dirt, are given the exalted honor of knowledge of God himself! The resurrection proved to the original witnesses that Christ is the Son of God; those witnesses passed this News on to their followers, and so it comes down to us today. Christ the Son is the Mediator, the meeting-point between God and man, and so through him we have access even to the Father himself.

Newness of Life

Christ's resurrection touches us directly today through the sacraments and through the teaching power of the Church, through which we receive our faith. The resurrection of Christ is the beginning, and its results are many and wonderful and varied, but ultimate goal of all of this is one: union with God.

No more is the "old man" that we were, the man of sin and straying, far from his Creator. The "old man" is gone in Christ; he was put to death and died, and the New Body of Christ, of which we become members through baptism, is renewed and placed above the possibility of death and of aging, neither physically nor spiritually. Though we were decrepit and rotting in the old age of our sins, Christ has made us young again in innocence and vitality through his Rising from the dead.

The Third Sunday
of the Resurrection

I will exult you O Lord, my King.

An ignorant and unwise people.

After your glorious Resurrection, an evil and deceitful people made centurions stand to guard your tomb. Woe to that unbelieving people! If they killed and buried, why were they standing guard? And if they were terrified of you, how did they dare crucify you? Indeed, your Resurrection on the third day has shamed your crucifiers, and gladdened your Church. Glory to you!

Reality Revisited

The "bare fact" of the rising of Christ and the evidence that supports it such as the empty tomb was stated and reflected upon by means of this hymn three weeks ago on Easter Sunday, as the second section of the Basilica Hymn for that greatest Feast of the year. The same hymn is repeated here, presented for our reflection a second time. A similar thing happened during Lent, when the same hymn was used during the first and last week, and we saw that the purpose there was to allow us to look at the same words with different, changed eyes, with eyes that had endured the battle and look back to its beginning matured and tempered from the fight.

The repetition here is of a different nature, I think. Here it is not so much a poem that is re-read at a different point in life and understood differently as a picture so marvelous that once seen, the viewer is forced by his own amazement to turn back and look at it again. He cannot take it all in by a single viewing. This is what we are doing during this Easter season: Christ is risen from the dead. The fact is so astounding that we must keep returning to it as a fact, not even as a source of poetic imagery or moral teaching, if we are to absorb its meaning as it deserves.

Mary Magdalene

Imagine having been there at the beginning, having witnessed Christ in his risen body, having received the Holy Spirit at that first Pentecost. Much more ordinary experiences call for reflection – a couple will watch their wedding video many times in their life, or visit the place where they first met, etc. But this earth-shattering event was so much more remarkable! How likely it is, then, that Mary Magdalene, who first visited the tomb and saw it empty, would have returned there many times to bring it all back to her memory afresh. And so, three weeks later, we return again to the empty tomb.

After your glorious Resurrection, an evil and deceitful people made centurions stand to guard your tomb. Woe to that unbelieving people! If they killed and buried, why were they standing guard? And if they were terrified of you, how did they dare crucify you?

Indeed, your Resurrection on the third day has shamed your crucifiers, and gladdened your Church. Glory to you!

The Fourth Sunday
of the Resurrection

Hear this, all you peoples.

In the doors of daughter Zion.

The cross was established in Jerusalem, and all creatures were gladdened; greedy death was unraveled in it, and the power of demons was taken away; it chased the Jews away to the four corners of the earth, and it gathered the nations together, and brought them into the Kingdom: that Paradise of heaven which Adam lost when he disobeyed, and the Second Adam conquered in Judah, returning its land to the Kingdom. He seized power in heaven and on earth, for behold, assemblies of angels worship before him, and they all cry out in one voice: thanksgiving to the Son of the Lord of All!

The Center of the World

The British having taken over a great part of the world in past centuries placed the "Prime Meridian," the "zero-point" of the globe, through Greenwich, London, effectively making themselves the "center" of the world, and the location of everything else in the world relative to them. "West" meant "west of London," and east meant "east of London;" the same goes for the still-used terms "middle east" and "far east." The Babylonians were the first to make such a bold declaration, and placed themselves in the center when they drew the first known map of the world. It is the trademark of any dominant culture to make itself the reference-point to which everything else is related.

For the Christian faith, it is not a city that is powerful in worldly terms that is the center, nor a place famed for its beauty or magnificence that is looked at as the reference for all around it. This is because the Christian faith is not about dominion or magnificence, but rather salvation. The Gospel is not about the sword taking over country after country by force, but about the redemption of the whole human race offered freely in the Blood of Christ. The Church is not about political force, but about the spiritual power of the Holy Spirit. Therefore, the center and focus of this new world is not London or Babylon, but the city of Jerusalem.

Universality

One momentary event in one city, the crucifixion of Christ in Jerusalem, makes waves all over the world: **"The cross was established in Jerusalem, and all creatures were gladdened; greedy death was unraveled in it, and the power of demons was taken away."** Its effects are not even limited to the physical world: death and demons are defeated by it. The authority of this new spiritual empire is wider than that of the empires of old, because it expands to the non-physical, and death, a concept, and demons, spiritual beings, become its slaves the way those conquered by the empires of old became its slaves.

Its expansion to the spiritual realm assumes that its expansion on earth is complete; the Gospel is preached not only to one nation, but to all, and the concept of Judaism is here made a symbol for exclusivity: "**it chased the Jews away to the four corners of the earth, and it gathered the nations together, and brought them into the kingdom:**" As opposed to a "national religion," we have now, because of the cross, an "international faith."

The Undoing of Adam's Defeat

The war that Satan fought against the human race began at its beginning, with Adam, and that first battle was lost by mankind. Because the battle was lost, earth, paradise and the human soul became the territory of the empire of the devil. But the cross, on which Christ shows how even God's weakest moment is mightier than Satan, fights the battle a second time: "**that paradise of heaven which Adam lost when he disobeyed, and the Second Adam conquered in Judah, returning its land to the kingdom.**"

At the creation, God gave Adam authority over the earth, to rule it in his Name: "fill the earth and subdue it..." This authority, though not entirely revoked, was made incomplete and impure at the moment when Adam and Eve sinned. No more did they completely speak in God's Name, because they had failed in keeping his commandment, and no more were they God's image in all purity. But the true Image of God, the Second Adam, came down to earth and obeyed in order to undo the first Adam's disobedience. Finally, the world has again one King, who is both God and Man, and who rules both heaven and earth: "**He took on authority in heaven and on earth, for lo, assemblies of angels worship before him, and they all cry out in one voice: thanksgiving to the Son of the Lord of All!**"

The Fifth Sunday
of the Resurrection

Praise the Lord from the heavens.
He turned the heavens and descended.

A servant descended from heaven, and shook the foundations of the earth; he made those who guarded you like dead men; and he strengthened the women who came to your tomb, and said: "Why do you cry, and why do you seek the one crucified by men, and buried like a man? He has risen above nature! Come and see the place where he was placed; he who has abounding mercies!"

Sight to the Blind

Our extended reflection on the Lord's resurrection, a reality that begins at the tomb and extends in resounding and echoing power till today, continues to develop in its insight. We began with the first witness, Mary Magdalene, and from her interaction with the angel, the tomb and the risen Lord our souls were imprinted with the power of the scene. As the reality of the resurrection begins to "soak in," we can look around and see everything else in its light, as if we were seeing for the first time. This new perspective on the world in light of the resurrection is not one we could ever reach with our own strength or intelligence; it is the graced sight of the eyes of faith.

127

From this angle, things look differently than they did before: we can see everything in a new way, with greater clarity and richness. Those who wear eyeglasses may remember the first time they ever put them on, and what a gift it was for them to do so, for it was as if the entire world was re-made just for them to gaze upon: every color was brighter, every line was straighter, every shadow was darker than it had ever been. Everything in the visible universe gained new meaning, and simply to look was a remarkable joy. This is not simply a Christian reality. Aristotle begins the Metaphysics with this reflection: "All men by nature desire to know. An indication of this is the delight we take in our senses; for even apart from their usefulness they are loved for themselves; and above all others the sense of sight. For not only with a view to action, but even when we are not going to do anything, we prefer seeing (one might say) to everything else. The reason is that this, most of all the senses, makes us know and brings to light many differences between things."

St. Paul, known as Saul before his conversion, was blinded after his first encounter with the Risen Christ. It was a "light from the sky" that began his meeting with the Lord, but when he opened his eyes, he could see nothing. It was not until he met a disciple, a member of the established Church named Ananias who laid hands on him, that "something like scales fell from his eyes and he regained his sight." (Acts 9: 18) We can be fairly certain that, from that point on, Paul never saw anything the same way again.

A Powerful Scene

Let us gaze, then, with our newfound sight, with our eyes of faith, at that first scene. At first, with human eyes, we attended to Mary Magdalene and her spices. We made note of the moved rock and the burial cloths. We discussed and debated the physical evidence for the Resurrection. We now look at the same scene, but believing. No longer do we debate whether or not he is risen, for some in the Church have seen him; no longer are the folded burial cloths so mysterious, for we know that he folded them himself; no longer is Mary Magdalene the central character. From the perspective of faith we can begin to see things, in some mysterious and small way, from God's point of view. How much more dramatic a scene is it from above, from heaven!

This is the approach our liturgy asks us to make this fifth Sunday of Easter, and the first phrase of our Basilica Hymn are meant to crash more loudly than the cymbals crashing at Mass and to resound more deeply than the rock rolled away from the tomb itself:

A servant descended from heaven, and shook the foundations of the earth; he made those who guarded you like dead men; and he strengthened the women who came to your tomb, and said: "Why do you cry, and why do you seek the one crucified by men, and buried like a man? He has risen above nature! Come

and see the place where he was placed; he who has abounding mercies!"

No more are the angelic beings fearful to us! Though they dwell in heaven, though they are powerful and invisible, they are now even servants! And, most amazingly, not only God's servants, but in some sense ours: this servant descended from heaven to tell us about the risen Lord.

The result of this new picture is a remarkable harmony: the angel came down to the natural world and shook it to its depths, in order to describe to us the One who has risen above all of nature, and an invisible being became visible to show us how to see the world, for the first time, as it truly is.

The Sixth Sunday
of the Resurrection

All who call upon his name will boast.
In the Lord is the boast of my soul.

We have gained an unending boast against death in the Cross of Christ, and in his Resurrection from among the dead. For by his suffering, he uprooted the sentence upon us. In great, unending glory, then, we all cry out and say: Only-Begotten God the Word, who assumed our mortal body, have pity, O Lord, on your servants, who confess in your Cross!

Bragging Rights

The devil's goal of forming our souls in his image is always accomplished through the sin of pride. Satan, in his extreme arrogance, refused to serve God and through this proud refusal fell from grace. In tempting us to do the same, he sometimes seems to "throw light" on certain aspects of our souls that we are proud of. But this is only an illusion; the devil is not a creature of light, but of darkness; he does not tell the truth, but is the father of lies. So what may appear to us as throwing light on our "good side," is in fact only a darkening of other things within us. The devil uses shadows to hide our sinfulness from us in order to let it grow, and uses distractions to make us forget our utter dependence upon God in order to plant the seed of pride. Thus the vice of bragging is doubly dark, because it covers up our sinfulness and ignores our weakness.

St. Paul, always a bold thinker, was weary of the boasting of those who pretended to follow the Law of Moses. He warns the Galatians that "It is those who want to make a good appearance in the flesh who are trying to compel you to have yourselves circumcised only that they may not be persecuted for the cross of Christ. Not even those having themselves circumcised observe the law themselves; they only want you to be circumcised so that they may boast of your flesh." (Galatians 6:12-13) The debate going on in St. Paul's time regarding the Christian observance of the Mosaic Law became a cause for pride for many, which in turn made the debate all the more heated. It became no longer a question of truth or justice, but of "my side" winning. But Paul snuffs his own pride on this question and returns the debate to the right arena: "But may I never boast except in the cross of our Lord Jesus Christ, through which the world has been crucified to me, and I to the world. For neither does circumcision mean anything, nor does uncircumcision, but only a new creation." (Galatians 6:14-15)

The Greatest Debate

Deeper than the argument between the first Faithful regarding the Law of Moses is that between humanity and the two criminal partners, Death and Sin. Adam had given in to Sin and become its slave, and Sin in turn sold him over to Death, and all of us with him. But Christ ransomed us from them and made us freemen and sons, and slaves no more. Such a difference in status between the first Adam and the second: "For the wages of sin is death, but the gift of God is eternal life in Christ Jesus our Lord." (Romans 6:23)

The final Basilica Hymn of the Easter Season, summarizing in one sublime expression all the joy of the Resurrection, brings all of this together:

We have gained an unending boast against death in the cross of Christ, and in his resurrection from among the dead, for by his suffering, he ended the sentence that was upon us. In great, unending praise, then, we all cry out and say: Only-Begotten God the Word, who assumed our mortal body, have pity, O Lord, on your servants, who confess in your Cross!

It is therefore with real confidence that we brag with St. Paul, who quotes the prophet Hosea: "Death is swallowed up in victory. Where, O death, is your victory? Where, O death, is your sting?" (1 Corinthians 55)

The Holy Feast
of the Ascension of Our Lord

O Lord, the God of my salvation.
You have arrayed him in honor and glory.

O Lord, in your love, you honored our nature: in the beginning, in your living image and in your likeness. And, because the Backbiter threw us out of our glory in his envy, you sent your Son. By his Birth, he turned our race back from ignorance; by his revered Baptism, he promised us adoption; by his suffering and death, he saved us from slavery to sin; by his Resurrection, he justified us, and by his Ascension, he lifted us up to his right hand.

The Mountain of the Lord

The 24th Psalm begins thus: "The earth is the Lord's and all it holds, the world and those who live there. For God founded it on the seas, established it over the rivers. Who may go up the mountain of the Lord? Who can stand in his holy place?" The Psalm continues in explaining that those who are pure and have a true faith will "receive blessings" from God, but it does not at any point answer its own question: Who may go up the mountain of the Lord?

In Biblical language, such an unanswered question is intended to have a negative answer. "Who is like the Lord our God?" in itself is meant to imply the answer "nobody." Similar also are many other questions in Scripture, such as "Who has understood the mind of the Lord?" and God's question to Job, "Where were you when I founded the earth?" (Job 38: 4)

Christ is the fulfillment of all the Scriptures, and the exception to every limitation placed on sinful humanity, and in fact, he is the one who has "climbed the mountain of the Lord" by ascending to heaven, an event which we celebrate on this Feast of the Ascension. The book of the Acts of the Apostles relates that Christ appeared to his disciples for a period of forty days before he ascended into heaven (Acts 1:3). Thus, forty days after celebrating his resurrection, we celebrate his ascending into heaven.

The View from Above

The perspective of the eye changes depending on its distance from its object as well as on the angle. The farther the eye is from the object, the less detail it can see, though its field of vision is wider. Similarly, the closer the eye is to its object, the more detail it can see, though there is less within its scope. On a merely human level, we can say that though looking at our life or our common history from far away deprives us of some detail; it allows us to single out the most important events and see them in relation to each other. In other words, because we cannot get caught up in the details of particular events, we are able to see only the most major moments. And this fact is not a consequence of our sins; it is a fact of our nature, with sin or otherwise.

The teaching of the Church is that Christ is fully human and fully Divine, even now while in heaven. That is, there was never a moment when his humanity was swallowed up or absorbed into his Divinity; the fact that he is God never took away from the fact that he is a man. That being the case, we must say, with all the teachers of the Church that even now, while in heaven, Christ has both a human and a Divine perspective, both a human and a Divine mind, the latter which is the Godhead itself, and the former which cannot ever comprehend it fully; if it did, it would cease to be a human mind at all.

The Basilica Hymn of the Feast of the Ascension is a human look at the events of salvation history. We know it is a human look, obviously, because it was written by a human being, but also because it has the limitation of the human mind: it is short and to the point, and within time and therefore limited in the amount of detail it can contain. Only the Divine Mind can at once view all of history in every minute detail. But even as a human examination of history, it is not one that is earthly, for its perspective is so wide as to imply an immense distance from its object. Perhaps it is a guess at the perspective of the Messiah who has ascended into heaven itself, who has climbed the mountain of the Lord and is looking down upon the whole physical realm in heavenly love, and who has brought us with himself:

136

O Lord, in your love, you honored our nature in the beginning, in your living image and in your likeness. And, because the Backbiter cast us out of our glory in his envy, you sent your Son. By his Birth, he turned our race back from ignorance; by his revered Baptism, he promised us adoption; by his suffering and death, he saved us from slavery to sin; by his Resurrection, he justified us, and by his Ascension, he lifted us up to his right hand.

The Sunday after the Ascension

He who was before the ages.

And his Name is before the sun.

God the Word, who, in his perfect Existence has increased his mercy toward our lowliness, has assumed our nature and united it to the *Qnoma* of his Divinity and bore the suffering of the Cross, that in his death he may give life to our race, and has ascended and taken his seat in heaven, above the princes and powers. Thus, as in the first Adam we had been condemned, in the second Adam we have conquered: and who can tell of his glorious age! Thus we glorify, and in knowledge believe, and in wonder confess, as he taught us in truth; nor indeed if even an angel from above were to come and speak to us, and alter his Gospel before us, beyond what has been preached to us, we will not deny his humanity, nor will we forget his Divinity.

Starting Over Again

Between the four Gospels, there are two distinct but complimentary approaches to presenting the Good News of salvation which occurred in the life of Christ. The first approach, which is utilized by the Synoptic Gospels (Matthew, Mark and Luke) is to begin with what is most obvious to the observer, the fact that Christ is a man, and to work from there to conclude decisively that he is also God. For example, Matthew and Luke, for different reasons, present the genealogy of Christ near the beginning of their Gospels to show the Lord's human background, but, through the course of their presentation, they make it clear that their main intent in writing (by the inspiration of the Holy Spirit) is to show the reader that Jesus is the Son of God. This dialectic formulation which works to prove something step-by-step and point-by-point is the most properly human way of thinking, but it is not the only one.

John's Gospel does not begin with what is most basic and obvious to us, but rather what is most basic and obvious to God. He does not start with the genealogy of Christ's legal human forefathers as does Matthew, but with his Divine Generation before the beginning of time: "In the beginning was the Word, and the Word was with God, and the Word was God." This is to see things, as we saw when we examined the hymn of the Ascension Feast, from God's perspective. This is to begin anew, even as Christ said we must be "born anew," to re-view human history and to see it, not through the suffering sinful eyes of those on earth, but through the loving and merciful eyes of the One who has ascended to heaven.

A Greater Richness

The Mesopotamian School, that is, the intellectual heritage of the Church of the East, has no complex about taking what is of value and making it her own. In theology and liturgy, she made many attempts to remain updated with developments happening in the West, for example by making certain to confess to the Creed of the Council of Nicea (a serious concern at the Council of Isaac in 410 AD), or by using the Trisagion (*Qaddysha Alaha*), a Greek hymn, in her liturgy. These are two among a multitude of examples that show that the true nature of the Church of the East is to be in union with, not in isolation from, the rest of the Christian Church.

Even more so, God has provided an abundant richness to his Church, and oftentimes a good thing comes to the whole universal Church through one particular tradition. That is why any authentic Apostolic Church must both be open to understanding its parallel traditions and receiving from them as well as to holding fast to everything it has in its own tradition, since God may again wish to give something to the whole Church through one particular Church. The Church of the East has received everything from Christ, and many things from other particular Churches, but I believe now is a time when she is to give to others by showing the Church Universal the treasures she has been keeping hidden for centuries.

The Gifts of God

A most unusual development in the history of the Faith is the misunderstanding and exaggeration of the word "alone." The popularization of such terms as "Scripture alone" or "faith alone" leads the mind of the believer to a minimalistic approach to the work of salvation, making it common experience to hear someone say "I don't need the Church when I have the Bible," or "I don't need the Sacraments when I have faith." What precisely is necessary in order to be saved is not my question here; such discussions are already abundant. Rather, what I wish to point out is the absurdity of the question itself. The question ultimately boils down to this: "What is the absolute minimum required for my salvation?" It is like a parent asking "what is the least I can do in raising my children?" or a husband saying "I have done X and Y for my wife, and that is sufficient. My job is done."

What manner of arrogance does it take to refuse a gift from God? What type of personality could watch the Creator of the world pour his graces out in a thousand ways and respond that "I only need this one, not the others." Why would God give us something we do not need? Faith is a gift from God – it is not a human endeavor, but the human mind accepting the freely given knowledge of God through the Holy Spirit. But faith is not the "only" thing Christ has given us; nor is the Bible. He has given us the Church; he has given us his Body and Blood; he has given us baptism; he has given us and continues to give us manifold graces in manifold ways. How could we reject a single one of them?

Even more, hasn't God given us an example to follow in being so unexpectedly abundant with us? When he has been so beneficent in providing graces, how could we be so cheap, both in receiving them and in giving good things to others?

The Point

The Basilica Hymn for the Sunday after the Ascension is an example of the Church of the East being expansive in her self-understanding and in her understanding of God's benefits. First of all, it is "Johannine" in nature, beginning with the eternal Existence of the Word of God. Secondly, it is one of the very few hymns that were adjusted when the Chaldean branch of the Church of the East came into re-union with the Catholic Church, in order to bring together the genius of the patrimony of the Church East of the Euphrates with the terminological and theoretical developments of the West, in a way concurrent with the drive of the Synod of Isaac and the other early Synods and liturgical developments of the Church. Finally, and most importantly, it is a reflection once again on the abundance of things that God has done for us in Jesus Christ the Son, and on the fact that nothing we do can even begin to repay the Lord for all his benefits to us. In fact our response can only be to "glorify, and in knowledge believe, and in wonder confess" the fullness of the Faith:

God the Word, who, in his perfect Existence has increased his mercy toward our lowliness, has assumed our nature and united it to the *Qnoma* of his Divinity and bore the suffering of the Cross, that in his death he may give life to our race, and has ascended and taken his seat in heaven, above the princes and powers. Thus, as in the first Adam we had been condemned, in the second Adam we have conquered: and who can tell of his glorious age! Thus we glorify, and in knowledge believe, and in wonder confess as he taught us in truth; nor indeed if even an angel from above were to come and speak to us, and alter his Gospel before us, beyond what has been preached to us, we will not deny his humanity, nor will we forget his Divinity.

The "dogmatic" nature of this hymn, that is, the fact that it is an affirmation of several articles of the Faith, does not prevent it from being intensely personal at the same time. In fact, the more deeply we look, the more we see that it is precisely the most "abstract" teachings of the Church that mean the most to us as individuals, and have the deepest impact on our direct friendship with God. Here, we have the Word taking on "our" nature, giving life to "our" race. Even more so, "we" are the ones who conquered in this Second Adam. In some marvelous way, then, we ourselves have ascended to heaven and sit at God's right hand, since it is our nature that he assumed.

Pentecost Sunday

The Lord will send his grace and his truth.

Before the Lord God, the Lord of all the earth.

The Holy Spirit who was sent from God, the Father of Truth, to the assembly of Apostles strengthened them by a graceful gift, encouraged their minds in his Gospel, and made their simplicity wise by his teaching through a multiplicity of tongues, that they may henceforth become ambassadors among all peoples, proclaimers of the kingdom of heaven, evangelists, and preachers of the Trinity.

Babbling

"The beginning" is always a mysterious concept because it is a reaching to the primordial, the time when things were not as they were now, and most of all the time which explains why now is the way it is. The beginning is a seed where everything later exists only in a hidden way, only in its potential. Who but an expert could guess, by looking at a mustard seed, what sort of plant it could grow into? And yet everything it becomes later is in the seed already, in its blueprint, in its capacity to become precisely this type of plant. Thus, the accounts of the beginning in the Bible are explanations of a fact already here, a plant that has already grown and, sometimes, already died and rotted out.

The eleventh chapter of the book of Genesis is an explanation of the fact that there are many different languages in the world. The story of the Tower of Babel is therefore one of the "seed" stories that show how the world became the way it is. "Now the whole earth had one language and few words..." A harkening to a wonderful past: not only was there lingual understanding between everyone alive, but also "few words," that is, perhaps, less of a need to explain, and less of a desire to talk about oneself. Mar Ephrem is quoted as saying that the wise man "talks little and listens much."

At any rate, this early innocence was lost when the people who had migrated to the land of Shinar (what we now call "Iraq") decided to build a city and a tower "with its top in the heavens," for the purpose of "making a name" for themselves. Their ultimate motivation, however, was a social one: they feared separation: "...lest we be scattered abroad upon the face of the whole earth." This human endeavor was not only a failure, however, but the very cause of the confusion found today. The attempt to force our way into the heavens, connected, in this primordial context, with "making a name" and preventing a scattering of peoples, caused the very thing they had feared. It says specifically that the Lord "came down" and that the final result was that he "scattered them abroad over the face of all the earth."

The Light of the World

The next time that the Lord "came down" in the context of languages was on the Jewish Feast of Pentecost, fifty days after the Resurrection of Christ. The account of this event is given in the second chapter of the Acts of the Apostles. The similarities between this account and that of the Tower of Babel are striking: the apostles were "gathered in one place" as the people of Babel had "settled" together; there was a "sound from heaven" as the Lord had "come down" from heaven. Most dramatically, the apostles "began to speak in other tongues," exactly like the people of Babel. Even the result was the same, for the apostles ended up going to the "ends of the earth" just as the people of Babel.

The difference, of course, is that the miscommunication caused in Babel was undone at Pentecost: the people of Babel became unable to communicate with each other; the apostles gained precisely that ability. Those who were there, hearing the apostles preach in so many languages, were people from all over the world (including also "residents of Mesopotamia," where the Tower had been built), and were amazed. The primordial separation of tongues which had forced the people of Babel to spread all over the earth was now fixed.

Moreover, the unwilling "spreading" of the people of Babel was replaced, not by a "coming together" of all the people of the world, but by another "spreading," one now done willingly, by the apostles. They became, as Christ had named them so much earlier, the "light of the world." That is, unlike the people of Babel, they were not interested in isolating themselves from the rest of the world; on the contrary, they took the Gospel to all nations and peoples. They realized that a lamp does not exist to brighten itself but others:

> **The Holy Spirit who was sent from God, the Father of Truth, to the assembly of Apostles strengthened them by a graceful gift, encouraged their minds in his Gospel, and made their simplicity wise by his teaching through a multiplicity of tongues, that they may henceforth become ambassadors among all peoples, proclaimers of the kingdom of heaven, evangelists, and preachers of the Trinity.**

Golden Friday

I will bless the Lord at all times.

And blessed be his honorable Name forever.

Blessed be Christ who came to suffer and die for us, who righted the fall of our race by the rising of his holy Body. And after his resurrection, he ascended to heaven, to his Sender, sits with him, to his right, and made his glory known to us through the gift of the Holy Spirit.

Participation

There are many times in Scripture when God is described as being "alone" in some attribute. St. Paul ends the Letter to the Romans by glorifying "God, who alone is wise..." In writing to Timothy (I Timothy 6:16-17), he speaks of God "the King of Kings and Lord of Lords, who alone has immortality..." Christ himself even says, after being called a "good teacher," that "no one is good but God alone." (Mark 10:18)

These are all true statements, but they say more than we think. Yes, God alone is complete Wisdom, Immortality, and Goodness (and many other things besides), but a further significance of this is that all of those who are partially wise or good come to be so by sharing in God's own Nature. Even partial wisdom exists only by a creaturely participation in God's perfect Wisdom; the same goes for our partial goodness, and even our existence. God, in creating us, in making us exist, gives us an analogous participation in his own perfect Existence – for it was he who said of himself, "I am who am." (Exodus 3:14)

This is all the more the case when we consider not only God's creative act but the even more abundant grace poured out through the sending of the Holy Spirit at Pentecost. In the Holy Spirit, which makes us not only distant and partial participants of the Divine Nature (by being created in God's image) but actual members of the mystical Body of Christ, we are all the more united with God's Life and participate all the more in his Nature and in his mission.

The Gifts of the Spirit

The Basilica Hymn for "Golden Friday," as it is called, describes this intimate connection between Christ's work, the Father, and the gifts of the Holy Spirit:

> **Blessed be Christ who came to suffer and die for us, who righted the fall of our race by the rising of his holy Body. And after his resurrection, he ascended to heaven, to his Sender, sits with him, to his right, and made his glory known to us through the gift of the Holy Spirit.**

The sequence of events is dramatic but incomplete: Christ came, suffered and died, rose from the dead, ascended into heaven, sits at the right hand of the Father (and we in him), and shows us his glory through the working of his Spirit. A wonderful summary of salvation history, but one that is incomplete and open-ended; one that begs the question: what are these gifts of the Holy Spirit?

The tradition of the Church has named seven gifts of the Holy Spirit, taken from Isaiah 11:2: "The Spirit of the Lord shall rest upon him, the spirit of wisdom and understanding, the spirit of counsel and might, the spirit of knowledge and the fear of the Lord." From this passage, the seven gifts named are: wisdom, understanding, counsel, fortitude, knowledge, piety, and fear of the Lord. But they are not simply inert, inactive, purely spiritual realities. They help us to act in a particular way.

Their Voice Was Heard throughout All the Earth

This is why the deeds of the apostles of Christ are so important for us to consider (indeed, this is why they are included in the Scriptures): when we see how they acted through the Holy Spirit, and how he acted through them, we learn more about the Spirit himself, and therefore about God himself. And so the Chaldean Church, on the Friday after Pentecost, celebrates a single but remarkable event in the lives of the two most important apostles: Peter and John. The story is related in chapter 3 of the Acts of the Apostles:

'Now Peter and John were going up to the temple at the hour of prayer, the ninth hour. And a man lame from birth was being carried, whom they laid daily at that gate of the temple which is called Beautiful to ask alms of those who entered the temple. Seeing Peter and John about to go into the temple, he asked for alms. And Peter directed his gaze at him, with John, and said, "Look at us." And he fixed his attention upon them, expecting to receive something from them. But Peter said, "Silver and gold I have none, but I give you what I have; in the name of Jesus Christ of Nazareth, walk." And he took him by the right hand and raised him up; and immediately his feet and ankles were made strong. And leaping up he stood and walked and entered the temple with them, walking and leaping and praising God.'

The name of this Feast, then, is taken from the phrase that Peter said: "Silver and gold I have none," making a subtle reference to the true treasure given to us by the Holy Spirit, the true power that is able to change the face of the earth and to heal the whole human race.

First Sunday of the Apostles

The Lord does whatever he wills.

Our God is in heaven, and he does whatever he wills.

The Holy Spirit, by his power, effects and does all things through his gifts: for he supplies prophecy, perfects priests in his grace, is able to bring wisdom to the simple (for to fishermen did he reveal the *Qnome* of Divinity), and in his power, he presides over the awesome liturgies of the Church. O Kin of the Glorious Nature! O Kin of the Adorable Inhabitance of the Father and the Only-Begotten Son! O Holy Spirit, glory to you!

The Spiritual Side

The gifts of the Spirit named in the book of Isaiah (11:2) are seven: wisdom, understanding, counsel, fortitude, knowledge, piety, and fear of the Lord. Notice that each one of these gifts is described is an interior reality – a virtue in the soul. The same is true of the fruits of the Spirit named in the Letter to the Galatians (5:22): "In contrast, the fruit of the Spirit is love, joy, peace, patience, kindness, generosity, faithfulness, gentleness, self-control."

Naming the gifts and fruits of the Spirit is the result of spiritual reflection upon the soul that has allowed the grace of the Spirit to work within its heart and change it into a new creature.

But as a reflection, it is a later reality; that is, this naming comes after the fact. The Spirit having come and having done his work, we look back and see what he has done within us.

The Physical Side

But in Scripture, the most immediate effect of the Spirit that is mentioned is a visible thing, rather than a spiritual reality or a virtue. The Acts of the Apostles (2:1-4) tell us that: "When the day of Pentecost had come, they were all together in one place. And suddenly a sound came from heaven like the rush of a mighty wind, and it filled all the house where they were sitting. And there appeared to them tongues as of fire, distributed and resting on each one of them. And they were all filled with the Holy Spirit and began to speak in other tongues, as the Spirit gave them utterance." The initial work of the Spirit, as related in Scripture, is a sound from heaven and an appearance of tongues of fire: a sound and an appearance, and then the apostles speaking in other languages. These are all physical realities, visible expressions of the power of the Spirit, rather than interior perfections of the soul.

This should tell us, among other things, that the work of God is never one-sided. Our sanctification in the grace of Christ is never only a spiritual reality; it has its manifest, physical aspect as well – if it did not, then it would seem to no purpose that "the Word became flesh." The physical manifestation of the Spirit comes about in our Christian life in many ways: in our moral life, in the social reality of the Church, and most of all in her sacraments.

The Gifts of the Spirit Revisited

The Chaldean tradition is always interested in the concrete expression of the Faith. Because the Word became flesh in order to communicate with us, she examines the "flesh" of the Faith with utmost seriousness. This is true of her deep and serious study of the Scriptures as well as her genius in the Liturgy, the physical expression of the Faith. Therefore, from her part, she might name the gifts of the Spirit from a different, concrete perspective:

The Holy Spirit, by his authority, effects and does all things through his gifts:

> **...for he supplies prophecy, perfects priests in his grace, is able to bring wisdom to the simple (for to fishermen did he reveal the *Qnome* of Divinity), and in his power, he presides over the awesome liturgies of the Church. O Kin of the Glorious Nature! O Kin of the Adorable Inhabitance of the Father and the Only-Begotten Son! O Holy Spirit, glory to you!**

The gifts of the Spirit named in this Basilica Hymn of the Second Sunday of the Apostles (the week after Pentecost), are therefore:

- the supplying of prophecy
- the perfection of the priesthood
- the instruction of the simple
- the liturgies of the Church

The prophecy referred to by St. Paul (1 Corinthians 14) for the building up of the Church is somehow intended to be an improvement on the reality of "speaking in tongues," since he prefers the former to the latter. The Chaldean Church, following his cue, makes the same point.

The priesthood of the New Covenant is also an improvement, since the priesthood of the Old Covenant was limited and ultimately ineffective. The true Priesthood of Christ, which is shared by all the faithful through their baptism (1 Peter 2:9), is the perfection of what was there before, and this is especially the case with the priesthood of the Apostles, which is the theme of the Basilica Hymn of the Third Sunday of the Apostles.

The instruction, or the giving of wisdom, to the simple is meant here very precisely to mean the knowledge of the Father, Son and Holy Spirit as three *Qnome* (a Chaldean word corresponding to "Person" in Western Trinitarian theology but best translated perhaps as "Individuality" or not at all) of one Divine Nature. It is remarkable as a work of the Holy Spirit because it allows the most simple of men to surpass the most educated in their knowledge of the highest Good.

156

Finally, the very rituals of the Church are so powerful to the faithful as to be inexplicable by merely human standards. In other words, there is no way to account for the Liturgy except by attributing its composition and performance somehow to the Holy Spirit himself. This is directly Biblical, of course, since the command to "do this" and to "baptize" was given by Christ himself, who is the one who sent us his Spirit, and without whom we would not have him within us.

Mar Addai

This Sunday also marks the Commemoration of the Apostle Mar Addai, one of the seventy disciples who came to preach the Gospel in our homeland between the rivers. As St. Paul says in the letter to the Romans, quoting Isaiah the prophet, "How beautiful are the feet of those who bring the good news!" (Romans 10: 15) With him we also celebrate one of the powerful preachers of the Gospel of Jesus Christ:

Precious in the eyes of the Lord our God is the death of his revered one, and the passing away of his saint, the honorable apostle. He who competed in spiritual battle in all excellence and left the divine arena in victory, leaving us a choice trophy, one excellent and spotless: his revered and honorable body. And lo, his soul processes with the angels, and offers prayers on behalf of our souls.

157

The two images used in this hymn are Biblical and, in fact, Pauline in nature. The first is the image of "fighting the good fight" or "running the spiritual race," which is found, among other places, in Paul's second letter to Timothy: "Bear your share of hardship along with me like a good soldier of Christ Jesus. To satisfy the one who recruited him, a soldier does not become entangled in the business affairs of life. Similarly, an athlete cannot receive the winner's crown except by competing according to the rules." (2 Timothy 2:3-5)

The second image comes not from Paul's writings but his deeds, which are described in Acts of the Apostles: "So extraordinary were the mighty deeds God accomplished at the hands of Paul that when face cloths or aprons that touched his skin were applied to the sick, their diseases left them and the evil spirits came out of them." (Acts 19: 11-12) The practice of honoring relics, that is the physical things that were near the saints or, as described here in Scripture, their skin itself, is one that our Church honors as well, and so our hymn calls the body of Mar Addai an "excellent and spotless trophy."

Of course, all of the honor due to saints and the power coming even from their bones is only a reflection of Christ and the grace he has poured out upon his body, the Church, and which comes to the human race through her, and so the final hymn commemorating Mar Addai ends as it should, with a glorification of the Master himself:

Blessed is your commemoration, O splendid apostle, who was persecuted for the sake of the Truth, and who endured pains and afflictions, that you may be an inheritor of the Kingdom. Who is able to describe the course of your spiritual works, which you prepared in vigil, fasting and prayer? May your prayer be a shelter for the sinners who take refuge in you, and may we be worthy to lift up glory to your Lord who has exalted you!

Shlyḥe

The Feast of the Body of Christ

Your Throne, O God, is forever.

I will magnify him and honor him.

Cherubim stand in fear and awe

before your throne, O Mighty One,

they hide their faces with their wings,

lest they behold that fearful sight:

lest their eyes see your Divinity,

the Fire that burns bright unceasingly!

And yet you, so glorious,

choose to dwell among mankind,

not that you may burn,

but that you may shine.

Great, O Lord, is your compassion,

and your grace, for you have visited our race!

Glory to the Father, to the Son and to the Holy Spirit.

Church, O betrothed of Jesus Christ

who saved you by his precious Blood;

gave you his Body (living Food

which wicked men had sacrificed),

who placed in your hands

his redeeming Cup

(his most precious Blood

that flowed from his side

when they stabbed him by the spear):

listen to the Bridegroom's voice:

repent, leave behind

vain wandering and sin.

Cry out to your Savior

with hymns of thanksgiving: "Glory to you!"

Exaggeration

Hyperbole takes cleverness; exaggerating to make a point is a creative endeavor. If not, if the exaggeration becomes cliché or faded with use, it no longer serves its purpose, and the point is no longer made. For example, when a woman is called "beautiful," and the same word is applied to a sunset or a painting, a new effort must be made if her beauty is to be complimented above these other things – she must be called "gorgeous" or "stunning" or some such thing, if the idea is to be expressed in an intense way.

But there is no way to exaggerate when talking about God. Every effort can and must be made, the mind must be exhausted of all its power, to tell even a fraction of his Goodness, and even then our language fails completely. The Third Anaphora of the Church of the East, attributed to Nestorius (but more likely composed by Mar Abba the Great), says it thus: "Who indeed is capable of telling the wonders of your Power, and of making all your glories heard? For even if all creatures became one mouth and one tongue, they would not suffice, O Lord, to relate your Greatness."

The Throne of God

The Bible stands up to this challenge superbly, as inspired by the Holy Spirit, and much of our language relating to God is derived from the Scriptures. For example, the author of the Letter to the Hebrews quotes Psalm 104 in addressing Jesus Christ, the Son of God: "You make the winds your messengers, and flashing fire your servants." This is a brilliant way to express the Greatness of God: by describing those below him as themselves great, the author is able to imply how much greater is God than they. Even his servants are so great that they are beyond the bonds of the bodily world. The angels are sometimes thus described as beings of fire, and the Chaldean tradition makes good use of this image. The first Anaphora, of Addai and Mari, calls them "ministers of fire and spirit."

Another image used in the Scriptures to "boost" our language of God is that of the throne. Psalm 47 connects the Throne image to the idea that God rules over all the earth: "God rules over the nations; God sits upon his holy throne." By describing this spiritual image as great and glorious, we are saying that even the thing upon which God is "sitting" is beyond our description in its greatness, and therefore so much more so is God. Imagining a great banquet, it is one thing to say that it was so splendid that the President was there; it is another thing entirely to say that the President was one of the waiters.

Fear and Trembling

The Basilica Hymn chosen for the Feast of the Body of the Lord, or *Corpus Christi*, is as ancient as any other in our tradition, though the Feast for us is relatively new, as it was begun in conjunction with the process of re-union with the Catholic Church a few centuries ago. But it brings together the extremities of reality and attempts to give some impression of the awe we should feel at the reality of the Eucharist:

Cherubim stand in fear and awe before your throne, O Mighty One, they hide their faces with their wings, lest they behold that fearful sight: lest their eyes see your Divinity, the Fire that burns bright unceasingly! And yet you, so glorious, choose to dwell among mankind, not that you may burn, but that you may shine. Great, O Lord, is your compassion, and your grace, for you have visited our race!

The second half, beginning, "And yet you, so glorious, choose to dwell among mankind, not that you may burn, but that you may shine," is precisely the point. God, in his overwhelming Greatness, has loved us enough to dwell among us in the Holy Eucharist.

The Bride

The Eucharist is given by Christ in a very precise manner; it is not like the Manna of the Hebrews, which simply fell from the sky. The Body of Christ comes to earth through the power of the

Holy Spirit, by the words of the priest who prays the liturgy of the Church. Thus the Bridegroom goes through a great deal to present his Bride with the greatest Gift he can give: himself. The Eucharist, then, is not an isolated reality. It exists and is given only for the sake of the Church, for her benefit, her sanctification, for her union with her Bridegroom. The second hymn used for this Feast is therefore addressed to the Church:

> **Church, O betrothed of Jesus Christ who saved you by his precious Blood; gave you his Body (living Food which wicked men had sacrificed), who placed in your hands his redeeming Cup (his most precious Blood that flowed from his side when they stabbed him by the spear): listen to the Bridegroom's voice: repent, leave behind vain wandering and sin. Cry out to your Savior with hymns of thanksgiving: "Glory to you!"**

The response of the Church to such a great Gift given by Christ is a clear one, and one which should become our own the closer we become to our Lord: listen to the voice of the Bridegroom, avoid sin, and cry out to Christ in praise and thanksgiving.

The Second Sunday
of the Apostles

Your priests shall be clothed with justice, your just ones with glory.
I will clothe the high priests with salvation, and the just with glory.
**The priesthood of the house of Aaron, in performing the law,
represented a mystery, a shadow and an image. But the
apostleship of the house of Simon received the embodiment,
the perfection, and the truth of the Incarnation. The Heir of
the Father loved that apostleship and by it he captured the
Earth. Indeed, by the hands of fishermen he returns and
captures the whole creation and, behold! it lifts up glory,
being baptized in the completeness of *Qnome* of the Father,
Son, and Holy Spirit – Glory to you.**

The Blood of Bulls and Goats

The Letter to the Hebrews is a sublime comparison of the
two Covenants between God and man. The first one, begun with
Abraham in a seminal form, was fully given to Moses at Mount
Sinai, and the second one completed in the sacrifice of Jesus
Christ. The nuances of the interrelation between the two
Covenants described in the Letter are too deep to explain here,
but a sort of summary of the Letter is found at the beginning of
Chapter 10: "Since the law has only a shadow of the good things
to come, and not the very image of them, it can never make

perfect those who come to worship by the same sacrifices that they offer continually each year." That is, the Law as a "shadow" of what was to occur in Christ was a preparation and an inferior copy, whereas the fulfillment was the "image" itself.

Of course the meaning of the ritual sacrifices of the Old Covenant either had to be pointing to something later as symbols, or they had no meaning at all; the same author assures us that "it is impossible that the blood of bulls and goats take away sins." No, those sacrifices were there only to prepare our hearts for their final fulfillment: that in his love, the Word of God became flesh and became a sacrifice on our behalf.

The Priesthood

The Hebrew word *cohen* (Chaldean *kahna*), which translates into the English "priest" is intended primarily to mean the priesthood of the Old Covenant, but its Greek equivalent *hierius* is used of Christ in its superlative *archierius* in Hebrews. In other words, Christ is a priest, not only of the Old Covenant, but of the New. The same word is also used by Peter in his first Letter as a substantive (*hierateuma*, "priesthood") to refer to all of the faithful in Christ: "You are a chosen generation, a royal priesthood." (1 Peter 2:9)

This term, however, is not used to refer to the apostles exclusively, or to any particular class of clergy within the Church. For this, a new Greek terminology was produced. At the top

166

were *episkopoi*, and those who helped them were *presbuteroi* and *deakonoi*. The first term, *episkopos*, literally means "overseer" or "guardian" and translates to the word "bishop." The second word, *presbuteros*, means "elder" and is the root of the English word "priest." The third term, *diakonos*, means "servant" and is the root of the English word "deacon." The Chaldean terms corresponding to these are *Episqopa* (a simple transliteration of the Greek), *Qashysha*, and *Mshamshana*.

Thus, those who were a class of leaders in the Christian community described themselves in different terms than those used for the old Jewish sacrificial system. But the point is there was still a class of leaders. Christ did not do away with earthly authority; it would take a blind reading of the New Testament indeed to not see that there is a difference between apostles and other disciples, that the two were charged with different duties, spoken to in different ways, and given different amounts of authority. This is one reason why the Christian tradition in general began to speak of the leaders of the New Covenant not simply in their own, newer, terms, but even as *hierioi*, that is, as a replacement of the old Jewish priesthood. In the Chaldean tradition, one is hard-pressed to find a reference to a *Qashisha* as a *Kahna*. But as the theology of the Church developed, the latter term was found fulfilled in the former.

The Basilica Hymn of the Third Sunday of the Apostles is an example of an early stage, but is a brilliant discussion of the two corresponding classes in the Old and New Covenants, the "priesthood" and the "apostleship:"

> **The priesthood of the house of Aaron, in performing the law, represented a mystery, a shadow and an image. But the apostleship of the house of Simon received the embodiment, the perfection, and the truth of the Incarnation. The Heir of the Father loved that apostleship and by it he captured the Earth. Indeed, by the hands of fishermen he returns and captures the whole creation and, behold! it lifts up glory, being baptized in the completeness of *Qnome* of the Father, Son, and Holy Spirit – Glory to you.**

Note well that the "embodiment, perfection and certitude" received by the apostles was not a doing-away of all ritual activity. The most basic "rubric" given by Christ is referred to here: at the end of the Gospel of Matthew, Christ charges the eleven to "go, therefore, and make disciples of all nations, baptizing them in the Name of the Father, and of the Son, and of the Holy Spirit, teaching them to observe all that I have commanded you." But this is not an empty, meaningless ritual, or even simply a symbol of something to come later. This is an "embodiment, perfection and certitude." This is a physical manifestation of the intangible grace that comes through the sacrifice of Christ; the expression of the priesthood of the New Covenant.

The Third Sunday
of the Apostles

The Lord is King, let the peoples tremble.
There they feared greatly.

O Lord, when the assembly of apostles was hidden, on account of fear and trembling from the Jews, from heaven the gift of the Holy Spirit descended upon them together. And in the four corners, they became preachers of your divinity and your humanity, and converted the whole creation from error, by the great power of the Paraclete; and we also, who take refuge in your grace, glorify you!

Objectivity

A large part of human life is a matter of opinion, as are many of our choices. The color of a new car, or what type of food to eat, and a multitude of such things are within the scope of taste and preference. But there are certain things that are outside of our choosing, and are true without needing our permission. Whether we like it or not, heavy things fall when we drop them. We can call this reality whatever we like ("gravity," for example), but the fact remains that it is a reality. No matter what our opinion or our preference, the fact is a fact, the truth is the truth.

169

Some truths are crystal clear, but others are the product of reflection and are not immediately perceptible to everyone, for many reasons. But that does not make them any less true. That a human being is best defined as a "rational animal" is either true or it is not; it may be a matter of debate, but it is not a matter of taste. The deepest truths can be the ones most difficultly arrived at, but they are the most important ones for the meaning of our lives.

The Light of the World

It is wrong to think that the most theoretical truths have the least practical application. It is not irrelevant, as some think, whether a human being is thought of as the image of God or as a mere collection of molecules. In fact, nothing could possibly have a more dramatic bearing on how we live on a daily basis. Equally relevant, even on a practical level, is how we think of God. Is he a loving Father who leads us gently to himself, who gave us his Son and his Holy Spirit, or is he a tyrant who commands us arbitrarily and looks forward to punishing us, or an angry figure who asks us to destroy those who do not believe in him, or does he not exist at all? The answer to this question will have an enormous say in every act of our lives, and in every choice we make.

That is why the question of faith is not a matter of opinion, because there is a truth – either there is a God or there is not; either we can know him or we cannot; either he cares about us or he does not. Again, though there is certainly room for debate, there is no room for preference or taste. Someone is right and someone else is wrong. This is why the Gospels do not speak of the message of Christ as "another opinion" or as a "good suggestion," but rather as "the light of the world." It is not even a matter of something "a little better," but of "light and darkness" or "black and white." The Gospel is a truth so deep and so drastic that it makes all the difference in the world.

The Basilica Hymn for the Fourth Sunday of the Apostles speaks of the apostles, after having been given the gift of the Holy Spirit, converting the whole world from error. Things were wrong, the mind of all mankind was convinced of a lie, and through the Holy Spirit, the world was made right and our minds were given the light of the Truth, who is the Person of Jesus Christ, who is True God and True Man:

O Lord, when the assembly of apostles was hidden, on account of fear and trembling from the Jews, from heaven the gift of the Holy Spirit descended upon them together. And in the four corners, they became preachers of your divinity and your humanity, and converted the whole creation from error, by the great power of the Paraclete; and we also, who take refuge in your grace, glorify you!

The Fourth Sunday
of the Apostles

The Lord will send his grace and his truth.
He will send from heaven and save us.

The Holy Spirit who was sent from above enlightened, instructed, and perfected the apostles; those who became, all of them, sowers of peace in creation, who drew open the shroud of gloom from the whole creation, and who preached heavenly renewal to peoples and nations. And while they endured constant scourgings from persecutors, that same Spirit strengthened them, and they prevailed and conquered every evil, and healed different diseases by his word. And while our Savior was with them as he promised from the beginning, they were exulting every day, wearing the sword of the Holy Spirit, and warring against the hordes of the tyrant, preaching true life.

A Review

The progress made in the liturgical calendar is a reflection of the history of the Church herself, and of all of salvation history. During Lent, our thoughts should move from selfishness to focus on Christ; during Easter, from the resurrected Lord to the heaven to which he ascended. How are our thoughts, and more importantly, the thoughts of the Church, progressing during this season of the Apostles?

Pentecost recalled the descent of the Holy Spirit, continuing the rhythmic movement of God's grace, shown in Jacob's ladder as angels moving "up and down." As Christ "went up," the Holy Spirit "came down" upon the Apostles in the upper room. The focus of the Basilica Hymn was the mission of the Apostles – having been given the Holy Spirit, now something is expected of them, and something great: the conversion of the whole world.

The Second Sunday of the Apostles named the gifts of the Holy Spirit in a very concrete, tangible way, revealing the personality of the Church of the East. The Spirit is not only an invisible breath or a lifeless shadow; it fills us with power and makes us work in manifest ways.

The Third Sunday reflected specifically upon one of the gifts of the Spirit: the "Apostleship of the house of Simon." In contrast to the priesthood of Aaron, this new form of leadership among the people of God, and especially this new form of ritual worship, is the real thing, rather than a mere symbol or foreshadowing of something to come.

The Fourth Sunday began to make clear the "movement" of this season from the upper room where the apostles received the Spirit to the world where they preached. It spoke of the error of the idolatry preceding the true faith, and of the grace of conversion given to the world through the preaching of the apostles.

The Spirit is Willing

Though each Sunday has led us more and more from the extraordinary experience of accepting the Spirit at Pentecost to the "nitty gritty" of the actual work of preaching in the world, thus far we have mainly seen the easy side of things. But being an instrument of Christ in preaching the Gospel is not always a walk in the park. The whole reason for the Gospel is that the world is in trouble; the whole reason for the medicine is that the world is sick, and this sickness is ugly indeed.

Even worse, oftentimes the medicine offered to cure the disease is bitter, and the sick person rejects it because of its bitterness, ultimately against his own interests. This puts the doctors in an awkward position – do they apply the remedy anyway and accept the anger of their patients, or out of selfishness do they give up on their patients in order to avoid their wrath? For the true disciple of Christ, the answer is clear – "Woe to me if I do not preach the Gospel!" (1 Corinthians 9:16).

The Battle Worth Fighting

This tension expresses itself ultimately as a kind of spiritual war, one primarily between Christ and Satan as the kings of their various domains, but one which reaches even the pawns on the battlefield, which we are. Nor does the battle reach its final minuteness in the battle between the Church and the sinful of this world, but even within the Church is there a struggle, as there is also within the soul of every person. The Lord's true battlefield is the individual soul; the victory to be won is the heart of each one of us.

It is Christ who fights, through his grace, for victory within us, so that he may dwell in us and we may belong to him. But he has chosen not to fight alone. He has sent his Spirit to his apostles that they may fight in his Name, and that same Spirit is with us today, fighting in two ways. First, the Spirit fights to win victory over our hearts, and secondly, he makes us his instruments so that he may win other souls as well. Luckily for us, both of these battles happen at the same time – as he fights for us, he uses us to fight for others; likewise, as he fights in others, he uses them to fight in us.

The Basilica Hymn this week is about this battle between light and darkness, and the role played by the apostles, and by us as well:

The Holy Spirit who was sent from above enlightened, instructed, and perfected the apostles; those who became, all of them, sewers of peace in creation, who drew open the shroud of gloom from the whole creation, and who preached heavenly renewal to

peoples and nations. And while they endured constant scourgings from persecutors, that same Spirit strengthened them, and they prevailed and conquered every evil, and healed different diseases by his word. And while our Savior was with them as he promised from the beginning, they were exulting every day, wearing the sword of the Holy Spirit, and warring against the hordes of the tyrant, preaching true life.

Commemoration of
Mar Shim'un Bar Sabba'e

O Lord, you search me and you know me

Choice silver that is tried in the earth

A portion of the heavenly treasure, which is desired by the angels, and by the prophets and apostles, and by the honored martyrs, Christ gave, in his grace, to the faithful Church: the venerable Mar Simon, he whose neck was sliced for the sake of the law of the love of God. Come, all you peoples, in awe and love, and in songs of the Holy Spirit, let us honor the day of his commemoration. He is indeed an unassailable rampart for our people.

A Story for Our Times

In the year 344 AD, by tradition on Good Friday, the bishop who held the See which would later be called the Patriarchate of Babylon was executed by the Persian emperor Shapur II. The events that led up to this are both touching and unfortunately all-too-relevant for our day.

Continually increasing tension between the Zoroastrian Persian empire and the Christian Roman empire worsened the relationship between the Christians of Persia and its king. King Shapur II, and especially some of his Magian advisors, began to see the Christians of his land as outsiders and spies, since they shared the religion of his enemy. The accusation, a false one, was that even the bishop of the empire's capital city Selucia-Ctesiphon, Simon, was personally a spy for Caesar.

The solution, it seemed to the Shah, was a double tax on his Christian population, since this would break the back of an already poor segment of the Persian empire. Even worse, he ordered that Mar Shim'un, the son of a garment stainer, ("bar Sabba'e"), was to collect the taxes himself.

The noble bishop refused, saying "I am no tax collector, but a shepherd of the Lord's flock." This is when the persecution became fierce. It became an excuse for the Shah to declare an open season on Christians, especially clergy who refused to follow the Zoroastrian practice of worshiping the sun.

Mar Shim'un was arrested and brought before the court, and given a devious offer: if only he alone were to deny Christ and worship the sun, all other Christians would be saved. This caused an uproar in the Christian community, which refused the offer of salvation through apostasy. In the end, king Shapur II, whom Shim'un had known since childhood, had the bishop taken out of the city of Susa with much of his clergy. Mar Shim'un had to watch as five of his brother bishops and one hundred of his priests were beheaded before him. Last of all, he was killed as well. The tradition says that all who were in line for execution sung, together, the hymn *Lakhu Mara.*

A portion of the heavenly treasure, which is desired by the angels, and by the prophets and apostles, and by the honored martyrs, Christ gave, in his grace, to the faithful Church: the venerable Mar Simon, he whose neck was sliced for the sake of the law of the love of God. Come, all you peoples, in awe and love, and in songs of the Holy Spirit, let us honor the day of his commemoration. He is indeed an unassailable rampart for our people.

What is it Worth?

In the eyes of the worldly, the Cross of Christ is ridiculous, as is the sacrifice it represents. To faithless eyes, the death of Mar Shim'un and so many faithful is a tragic and meaningless waste. It would seem so logical to ask "were it not better for the patriarch to apostasize, or for the Christian segment to rebel against the empire and start a war, or to flee, or to do anything besides offer their lives in sacrifice?" This is a flawed logic both in the eyes of faith as well as in the practical world. There is no reason to believe any such thing could have prevented the "Great Persecution" which followed Mar Shim'un's death; nothing would have been gained, and the faith would have lost its integrity.

But what if it would have helped, in some practical way, for the Patriarch to give in, to hide from his responsibility to preach the Gospel and be a witness to his Lord? What would have been traded for this worldly gain? What gain is worth apostasy?

What can replace the Faith? "What can one give in exchange for his soul?" (Matthew 16:26)

The real question, rather, is "How much is the faith worth?" The answer can only be "everything." If it is not worth everything, every sacrifice and every suffering, then it is worth nothing. It is either the Truth, for which even pagans were willing to sacrifice their lives, or it is a lie, which deserves our scorn. If the Faith is true, if the Church is real, if Jesus is Lord, then they deserve our lives. This is what Mar Shim'un understood, and what we have perhaps forgotten today.

Would we give our life for our faith? Or would we find some excuse for ourselves? Would we live according to what we have been taught by the Holy Spirit, or would we ignore it all for some passing worldly wisdom? How much is Christ really worth to us? If we do not know the answer to these questions, perhaps we should ask Christ to show us ourselves.

O Knower of the thoughts of all men, and Searcher of the hidden things of the heart: you know our weakness: have mercy on us.

A Piece of Poetry

The Presentation Hymn set for New Sunday, the first Sunday after Easter, is attributed to Mar Shim'un bar Sabba'e, and it is about those newly baptized the week before, during the Easter Vigil, removing their white garments after wearing them all week. But it is not simply a calm piece of advice to the new batch of Christians. Its terms are intense and its warnings severe; it speaks of Adam and Satan, of temptations and the armor of the Spirit; it is the type of poetry one writes during a persecution. The language and subject-matter of this piece suggest that it really was written during that early time of persecution, which means that perhaps the attribution to Mar Shim'un is an accurate one.

In any case, the hymn is beautifully written and its images are as potent today as they ever were; its message is as meaningful for us as it was for those Christians executed one by one in the sight of the bishop of the Persian capital city:

> Even if you strip off your outer garments,
> do not take off your inner vestment, O Baptized!
> Indeed, if you are clothed with this hidden armor,
> the storm of many temptations will not defeat you.
> You know what words you have heard;
> you know of what living Sacrifice you have eaten.
> So beware the evil one, lest he entrap you as he did to Adam,
> and make you strangers to that glorious kingdom;
> for he estranged [Adam] from Paradise,

and wishes also to estrange us.

Because of this, then, implore Christ with us,

that he may confirm all our souls through his Holy Spirit.

The Fifth Sunday of the Apostles

The Lord is faithful in his words.

His word is complete unto the ages.

**O Lord Jesus Christ, you completed and verified the Promise
of the Father, promised by means of your holy disciples. They
accepted the gift of the Holy Spirit; they went out, made
disciples of and baptized the peoples and nations, by means
of varying tongues and turned them to the knowledge of God.**

The Promise

As an author, St. Luke is highly interested in the
fulfillment of promises. He begins his Gospel with the promise of
the angel to Zechariah. Zechariah's initially negative response to
the angel's assurance of what is going to happen becomes an
occasion for a strict punishment. Going against God's promise,
refusing to take part in it, requires a harsh penance.

The common element, the link, between Luke's Gospel
and his second book, the Acts of the Apostles, is also a promise.
After the resurrection, the last thing Christ says to the disciples
before ascending to heaven is "behold, I am sending the promise
of my Father upon you; but stay in the city until you are clothed
with power from on high." (Luke 24:49) This word is fulfilled at
the beginning of Acts, when the Holy Spirit comes upon the
disciples in chapter 2.

If Luke is so concerned, then, with the promise of the Father, his concern is really with explaining the Holy Spirit. The concept of "covenant," meaning (in Scripture) an agreement or a promise between God and man with the purpose of uniting the two, is fulfilled to its fullest earthly extent in the giving of the Holy Spirit. It is in him that we believe in Christ. It is he who makes this group of people into the Church. It is through his power that the Body of Christ comes to earth upon the altar. It is he who allows the Bride to be united to her Bridegroom.

The Commission

Though the grace given through the Spirit is totally free, that is, is both unearned and unrepayable on our part, it is not given to be hidden or greedily tucked away. God wishes his grace to be brought to the ends of the earth. In other words, the union of the heavenly Bridegroom and his Bride is not meant to be fruitless or childless – the Church is to give birth to many spiritual children.

This ultimate gift of God, then, the Holy Spirit, is one that God expects us to use for the good of the whole human race, and the Spirit's dwelling within us is an empowerment and a strengthening meant to drive us to become instruments in God's own work. We are given a gift which gives us a mission, and this mission is the sanctification of the world which comes about by the conversion of the nations; those who do not know God are brought to him.

Hands

God's presence in the world is therefore extended and increased the more he dwells within the hearts of men, for it is only there that there is true spiritual darkness, and only there that there is true moral evil. We disciples of Christ, whose mission it is to spread the Light of the Gospel, become the very hands of God, therefore, when we take part in God's work. It is no longer our old selves working for our own agenda, with our own motivation and our own strength. This is a miserable state of life, for it leaves us totally alone in the end. No, now it is not so much we who work but Christ in us, through the Spirit:

O Lord Jesus Christ, you fulfilled and verified the Promise of the Father, promised by means of your holy disciples. They accepted the gift of the Holy Spirit; they went out, made disciples of and baptized the peoples and nations, by means of varying tongues and turned them to the knowledge of God.

The Sixth Sunday of the Apostles

God will send his grace and his truth.

He will send from heaven and save us.

The Spirit, the Paraclete, is the Power that is from the Father and the Son, who dwelt in the Apostles, the friends of the one who gives life to all, and made them the salt which seasons the taste of the dull. They enlightened the world through their teaching, and gained clarity. They believed and confessed in the Father, the Son, and the Holy Spirit. And while Satan marshaled his armies for battle, they did not tremble from afflictions, nor were they weakened by torments; for by the suffering and death of the Son were they saved, and because of this, they gave their flesh over to accept every torture, that they may resemble their Lord. For they saw that by his suffering he saved his Church, and by his death he gave life to all creatures, that they may become, for him, heirs of the kingdom.

Theory

The Greek word *theoria* means "looking" or "observing." It is, both in ordinary language and in the understanding of the Fathers, the compliment and even contrary of "practice" or "action." The dynamic between these two relative expressions in the Christian faith is symbolized in Luke's Gospel in the passage about Martha and Mary. While Mary sat at the Lord's feet and listened to him speak, Martha was busy and anxious with housework.

The tension between prayer and action is a common one in Christian life, but the solution is not a simple matter of balance. Mary, in Christ's words, "chose the better part" (Luke 10:42). The two are not equal sides of the same coin. Neither is it right that, even worse, prayer and rest, "sitting at the Lord's feet" as it were, exists for the sake of action, as if we pray only in order to be "energized" for our work in the world. This is, unfortunately, the view most common in the world – especially in America – about rest and vacation. One today does not work so that he has a time and place to rest well; he rests only so that he may work more efficiently. This is a sad state of life, and contrary to the expectation that Christ has for us: "the Sabbath was made for man, not man for the Sabbath." (Mark 2:27)

The greater thing in human life, the "better part," is *theoria* or observing the goodness of the Lord and of the world he has made. The deeper this observing becomes, the more we live out our lives as God's true children in Christ. The more we observe God's own Nature, the more we know him and become like him. This is why the first part of the Basilica Hymn of the Seventh Sunday of the Apostles is a reflection on the interior Nature of the Holy Trinity:

The Spirit, the Paraclete, is the Power that is from the Father and the Son...

But, just as *theoria* is not the whole picture of Christian life, neither is simply the theoretical understanding of the Trinity the whole picture of salvation history.

Seasoning Salt

The Lord asks a pointed question near the beginning of the Sermon on the Mount: "if salt loses its taste, with what can it be seasoned?" Even more pertinent perhaps is what can give us taste if we already find ourselves bland? Our hymn answers this question:

> **...who dwelt in the apostles, the friends of the one who gives life to all, and made them the salt which seasons the taste of the dull.**

It is this same Holy Spirit who is the Power from the Father who dwells in the apostles and in us, and makes us the salt of the world which Christ asked us to be. It is through the Power of God in the Holy Spirit that salt is seasoned, that it is made into salt.

As a consequence, the apostles lived a life of service and action, becoming the "light of the world" though they were foremost in the knowledge and intimacy of God that comes through a silent, meditative observation:

They enlightened the world through their teaching, and gained clarity. They believed and confessed in the Father, the Son, and the Holy Spirit.

The two elements of action and meditation are intertwined here, not as a result of human effort, but rather as a result of the work of the Holy Spirit: the apostles enlightened the world at the same time as they confessed the Trinitarian Mystery.

In fact, and this is the main point, they enlightened the world *because* they confessed the Trinitarian Mystery. Their work was a direct consequence of their meditation, a natural, almost effortless and certainly spontaneous expression of their "observation" of God in heaven. In other words, the world did not gain flavor and light because of *what they did*; they became the salt of the earth and the world became flavorful and enlightened because of *who they were*. Our hymn does not say that the Holy Spirit "gave them flavor," but rather that it "made them the salt of the earth." So with us, if our action is to be a true expression of our faith, and if it is even to be truly effective, it should be more a result of who we are because of God dwelling in us, and less of what we do by our own human effort.

Holy War

Who are the real enemies of the Christian faith? More pertinently, who are the real enemies of Christians, and how are Christians supposed to fight them? The concept of a holy war is

189

one that has never existed for the Church of the East, the Church east of the Roman Empire, which never had an army with which to fight.

On the other hand, the concept of "spiritual battle" as the soul's fight against the devil and its own evil inclinations is one common among the writings of all the Fathers of the Church. But even here there is a nuance worthy of consideration: the spiritual battle is not merely spiritual, just as our meditative *theoria* is not closed off, even by its own nature. There is a physical element to the spiritual battle, one which shows itself to the world and brings it light and hope: not the fight of the sword, but martyrdom. Martyrdom, the giving of one's blood for the faith, is the ultimate victory of spiritual battle against the true enemy, the devil, and it is the ultimate victory because it is the ultimate imitation of Christ, who gave life to us all by his death:

> **...And while Satan marshaled his armies for battle, they did not tremble from afflictions, nor were they weakened by torments; for by the suffering and death of the Son were they saved, and because of this, they gave their flesh over to accept every torture, that they may resemble their Lord. For they saw that by his suffering he saved his Church, and by his death he gave life to all creatures, that they may become, for him, heirs of the kingdom.**

Memorial of the 72 Disciples

Their Gospel goes out to all the earth.

They walked from nation to nation.

O holy apostles, who preached and taught the new Gospel in the four corners, uprooted the thorns that the evil one planted through his weeds, planted good seed by means of their teaching, and fulfilled and completed the charge they accepted, and transmitted this to the teachers and priests: O victorious athletes, O true pillars, supplicate and plead to Christ for peace!

The Garden

Dirt is ugly alone, but what it produces can be beautiful. The reason it is ugly, however, is not because of its color or texture, but because of its blandness, its uniformity. It is all the same, without variety, and where there is no variation, there is no physical beauty. But as a potentiality, simple dirt contains all the beauty of the most stunning gardens.

Even gardens can vary in their beauty; there are many types of plants, and a selection and arrangement may be more or less well done. Flowers of a certain color may look better next to others or not; trees bearing one fruit may accentuate others or hurt their look. Much of the work of creating beauty is precisely in this ordering. But one thing is certain: the most beautiful gardens do indeed have a great variety of plants, and not just one kind; otherwise, the view would be more like that of simple, uni-colored dirt than of a true garden.

Such is the garden of the Church, which contains many kinds of expressions of beauty, many attempts to flower forth for the glory of God. Within the Church, there are many Rites, many different traditions, many different devotions, each having its own beauty and contributing to the beauty of the whole. If all were reduced to one, the Church, the Garden of God, would lose a great deal of her beauty: if the whole Church were only the Latin Rite, for example, or if its only devotion were the Rosary, and there were nothing more, there would certainly be something and something of great value, but not the gorgeous beauty we have before us today. Something enormous would be lost.

The same is the case with the garden of the human soul: there is so much in man that is complex and mysterious, so many interlocking pieces within him that make him stand out above all other creatures. And again, much of his beauty would be lost if he were made more autonomous or more simple, even if this would make his life "easier" in some shallow way. Imagine how much less suffering there would be if man were only a spirit without a body; there would be no disease or death, but neither would there be the drama of communication and interaction. Imagine how much simpler the world would be if man had no free will: there would be no sin! But neither would there be love, or charity, or justice.

The Work and the Workers

Any gardener will testify, however, that the real work of making a beautiful garden is not in the selection or in the variety. That is an initial decision that is done with delicacy and is maintained, but not a constant trial. No, the real work of gardening is in ripping out the weeds. Yes, there is a variety and many different plants have their place in a garden, but not weeds. Though there is variety in the Church and in the soul, the true beauty of both comes out fully when evil is ripped out by Christ, who was at first mistaken for a gardener by Mary Magdalene just after he rose from the dead (John 20:15).

Christ's mission is extended in the work of the Apostles and their successors, and they continue to work within the souls of the faithful by the grace of Christ. Though the work of pulling the weeds out of the world is a job reserved for the angels (cf. Matthew 13:39), Christ reaches the weeds within our souls through his instruments in his Church:

O holy apostles, who preached and taught the new Gospel in the four corners, uprooted the thorns that the evil one planted through his weeds, planted good seed by means of their teaching, and fulfilled and completed the charge they accepted, and transmitted this to the teachers and priests: O victorious athletes, O true pillars, supplicate and plead to Christ for peace!

The Holy Feast
of the Twelve Apostles

Their gospel went out to all the earth.

They kept his witness and the covenant he gave them.

The holy apostles taught one perfect confession by the Holy Spirit, and uprooted and banished from the earth the thorns and weeds the evil one had planted in the world. They planted, instead of them, the seed of their teaching. With the light of their words, they quenched and destroyed the darkness of error that had seized the world. They preached the true faith through all the inhabited world, in the adorable Name of the Father, the Son, and the Holy Spirit, the Nature that is incomprehensible!

To Tell the Truth

A cynic may ask what difference it makes what people believe: why should the belief in one God, for example, have any real impact on someone's life or happiness? The pagan and the Christian live in the same world, see the same things, even (in many cases) live similar lives. A pagan can be a good husband and father, a model citizen and a fine worker. He can look around himself and see the beauty of the world, appreciate it with depth and love, and even write poetry about it. Even assuming he were believing a lie, how different would his life be if he believed in one

God instead of many? Even more so, how different would his life be if he believed not only in the one true God, but also in the Son of God, the Messiah foretold by the prophets?

This points to a larger question: how is truth itself of greater value than falsehood? On the basic human level, this question is ridiculous: of course knowing the truth in itself is a better thing than believing a lie. But we are not dealing with the basic human level here, but something strange and exceptional, something with the hint of the inhuman; we are dealing with the cynic.

To answer the cynic, then, the wise man would do well to scrape the surface of the cynic's question: why is it asked and how could it be otherwise? That is, what assumption does the cynic have that leads him to question the very value of the truth? Is it really true that the pagan's happiness, though lived in a lie, is equal to the Christians? Yes, he may perform similar activities, have similar relationships and share in some sort of natural joy, but is there nothing more to the life of a human being?

We must remember that this question is not asked to empty air, but to a human being, to you and me, and when the cynic asks us what value is our knowledge of the truth he is implying something about us, and that this implication is insulting. He is implying that human life is nothing more than eating and drinking, enjoying simple things and then dying. This is a fine life for a cow, but not for man. Man is not just another mass of cells temporarily alive; man is a mind and a will; man is an image of God, and thus man is thirsty for something more than food and drink.

Weeds

Knowledge of the truth is a nourishment that, from the whole physical world, can only be enjoyed by a human being. To know what is and what is not is only for us, whereas other living things share most of our other joys and pains. That is why the truth is so important: it is what makes us human beings, and why a lie is so harmful: it is what corrupts the greatest thing within our being. That is the difference.

Unfortunately, there are many lies and there can only be one truth. That is why the Lord compares the world to a field containing many plants, some wheat and some weeds (Matthew 13). This description of the commixture of truth and falsehood in this world, of good and evil, gives us an insight into even the practical good of knowing the truth: the difference between truth and falsehood is the difference between wheat and weeds. Wheat is fruitful and self-sustaining, and pleasing to the eye. Weeds, on the other hand, are fruitless, choke other plants, and ugly. The truth also is fruitful – it produces good in the world; it is self-sustaining and does not rely on anything else for its existence and flourishing; it is beautiful. But falsehood is none of these things, and notably the very falsehood of cynicism: it produces no good for anyone; it thrives only in attacking other things; and it is ugly.

The weeds of falsehood and idolatry are the work of God's enemy the devil, and it is these weeds that attempt to choke the truth of the Gospel entrusted to the apostles. But the ultimate Truth is Jesus Christ, the Light of the World, who cannot be overcome or even comprehended by darkness. Through all trials and tribulations, against every work of darkness and every weed, the true faith will always prevail:

The holy apostles taught one perfect confession by the Holy Spirit, and uprooted and banished from the earth the thorns and weeds the evil one had planted in the world. They planted, instead of them, the seed of their teaching. With the light of their words, they quenched and destroyed the darkness of error that had seized the world. They preached the true faith through all the inhabited world, in the adorable Name of the Father, the Son, and the Holy Spirit, the Nature that is incomprehensible!

The First Sunday of Repentance

O Lord, do not reproach me in your wrath.
I became like a wasted vessel.

O Lord, it is not from this present life that I profit in greatness of my sins, nor is it from that which is eternal, due to the faults that are stronger than I. In shamefacedness do I stand on the day of judgment, as I tremble and groan forever, without escape. I call your mercies to come to my aid, O Lord, that on the day of your coming, you may forgive my sins, and have mercy on me!

Profit

Much of the Wisdom Literature of the Old Testament comes to us in the form of a tirade against the misery of this passing world. The Book of Ecclesiastes begins, "Vanity of vanities, vanity of vanities! All things are vanity! What profit has man from all the labor which he toils at under the sun?" The cry of the prophet, so full of vigor and emotion, can be used as a kind of tuning-fork against our own souls: what is our reaction when we hear his cry? What is our response when someone questions the value of "all things?" Is this prophecy another expression of the cynicism we discussed last week?

The spiritual atmosphere of the Bible, and therefore of the Church, is a refined mixture of varying attitudes toward this world and life within it. On the one hand, we have the certainty that this world, as it is created by God, is "very good," and is declared to be so by its Creator in the book of Genesis. On the other hand, we have the passage above and dozens of others seeming to question the very value of this world. Even Christ himself shows such a refined approach to this world, using, on the one hand, so many examples drawn from nature and telling us to "look at the birds of the sky" (Matthew 6:26), and only a few verses before commanding, on the other hand, that we "store up treasures in heaven, where neither moth nor decay destroys, nor thieves break in and steal." (Matthew 6:20)

The key to understanding this, the rationale behind the refinement, is the concept of "profit." It is true that this world is good and beautiful, that it is in place for our enjoyment and delight in the Creator, but it is not something beyond us. On the contrary, the Basilica Hymn of the Fourth Sunday of Lent discusses how it is somehow contained within us: not only are we a part of it, it is a part of us. Gaining it, therefore, is to gain nothing more than we already have. Indeed, Christ even asks, "What profit is it for a man to gain the whole world and forfeit his life?" (Matthew 16:26). The whole world is worth exactly what we are, and certainly not more, and so to gain it and all its pleasures is to retain our net worth, but to make no profit at all.

It is the human drive to find something more, something more real, more valuable, more wonderful that makes us desire and that makes us human. This need is confused when it thinks that this "more" is to be found in this world, and disappointed when it looks there and does not find it. "More" is found in Christ himself, the union of God and man and of heaven and earth, who came that we may "have life, and have it more abundantly." (John 10:10)

Two Faces

In the eighteenth chapter of the Gospel of Luke, we are given two paradigms for our relationship with God, one good and one bad: "Two people went up to the temple area to pray; one was a Pharisee and the other was a tax collector. The Pharisee took up his position and spoke this prayer to himself, 'O God, I thank you that I am not like the rest of humanity – greedy, dishonest, adulterous – or even like this tax collector. I fast twice a week, and I pay tithes on my whole income.' But the tax collector stood off at a distance and would not even raise his eyes to heaven but beat his breast and prayed, 'O God, be merciful to me a sinner.'" (Luke 18:10-13)

After having realized the emptiness of this world, it would seem that the natural thing to do would be to look to the world beyond, but surprisingly it is not so simple. It is the Pharisee who faces "up," presumably toward heaven, and the tax collector who "would not even raise his eyes to heaven." Christ condemns the attitude of the Pharisee as arrogant and inappropriate before God,

201

and praises the spirit of the tax collector. Where should we be facing? Is it enough to be simply unsatisfied with this world and want heaven? Is heaven something we can steal, a palace we can storm, simply with the force of our desire and feeling of deserving? Christ's answer is no, and this answer points us to another reality in addition to the "vanity" of this world: the reality of sin. Factoring sin into this equation we realize that things are much worse than we thought: not only must we look beyond this world to find fulfillment, we must look beyond ourselves as well, toward Christ and his forgiveness. Not only are we empty without the higher reality of heaven, we are wounded and sick and cannot even enjoy the partial pleasures of this world without his mercy.

Even without the reality of sin, placing our hopes upon this world is frustrating and ultimately empty. But when sin sneaks in, all the more must we reach out to what is beyond this world – to the One who is beyond this world – not only for fulfillment, but even for healing and forgiveness. The Basilica Hymn of the First Sunday of Repentance summarizes these ideas succinctly and powerfully in the form of a prayer to the Lord, remembering how little profit there is in this world, recalling its end and the Day of Judgment, and expressing the attitude of the tax collector who was made a model for all of us:

O Lord, it is not from this present life that I profit in greatness of my sins, nor is it from that which is eternal, due to the faults that are stronger than I. In shamefacedness do I stand on the day of judgment, as

I tremble and groan forever, without escape. I call your mercies to come to my aid, O Lord, that on the day of your coming, you may forgive my sins, and have mercy on me!

The Second Sunday
of Repentance

My legs were standing within your gates, O Jerusalem.
And my life reached Sheol.

You stand at the doorway of the end of your life, O my miserable soul! Indeed, here you have occasion to beg for forgiveness, but there tears will not profit nor repentance aid—when the Bridegroom enters, and all his guests enter with him, and he closes the doors, and the veil is drawn. Who, therefore, is my hope, aside from you, O Lord? O Lover of mankind, O God, forgive me!

Assumptions

A great deal of modern thought is concerned with looking behind opinion and belief, the things that are "assumed" by most people, and examining these assumptions critically. This is a noble endeavor if its goal is to discover the truth, but its scope should not be simply opinions and beliefs; this is ultimately stale and inhuman. Looking critically at assumptions, questioning already-held beliefs, should first of all be an intensely personal mission; we should question first ourselves, not only our ignorant opinions. The question we should ask first is not "how do I know?" but "what am I?" This is a more logical starting-place and the road it begins is more intellectually secure.

If this is the most primordial question, then the most commonly held opinion is in answer to it. Socrates found frustration in this, because his opponents made an assumption that he did not: his opponents believed they knew, and that they were good and just. The opponents answered the question "who am I?" by saying "I am a good person" "I am a wise person" or "I am a just person." It generally took Socrates minutes to destroy this assumption, to show his opponents they did not know what they thought they knew.

The Christian Faith is the sharpest, most critically refined mode of thought because rather than assuming a falsehood, it answers this first question correctly. If the question is "what am I?" the Christian's answer is "I am a creature of God and his image, but a sinner." This delicate answer instills caution in every further question, because it assumes that we are weak and need to proceed very carefully, because of how easily we can fall.

The Hallway and the Door

There are many ways to err, but only one Truth; there are many paths in this life, but only One which leads to salvation. In the terminology of the Gospel, Jesus Christ is himself both the Truth and the Way to get there. But it is so easy to fall into the temptation to try other paths which perhaps seem easier or more pleasant. The way that is Christ is challenging; it is an exercise and a sacrifice; it requires becoming a new creation, throwing off our old selves and allowing God to make us alive in a different way through his Son. This can be intimidating and scary, and in our weakness and attachment to our old selves we can reject this path and continue on our own path, leading to our isolation from Christ and ultimately our destruction.

We must realize who we are before we begin to walk; we must realize how miserable and empty we are alone, if we are ever going to become something new. We must acknowledge that the path of our own selfishness is one that is full of traps and unseen potholes, a dark and ugly road that leads to nothingness, the nothingness out of which we were created. Knowing this, knowing who we really are, will turn us toward the true Path, and we will trust in him rather than in ourselves.

Our choice is now, not later. This is the time to turn to the Lord, to put our selfishness and arrogance aside. This is the time to see ourselves weak and wounded, and turn and be healed. This is the time to obey the commands of the Lord and make ourselves known to the Bridegroom, lest he tell us he does not know us:

You stand at the doorway of the end of your life, O my miserable soul! Indeed, here you have occasion to beg for forgiveness, but there tears will not profit nor repentance aid—when the Bridegroom enters, and all his guests enter with him, and he closes the doors, and the veil is drawn. Who, therefore, is my hope, aside from you, O Lord? O Lover of mankind, O God, forgive me!

The Third Sunday of Repentance

Turn to me and have mercy on me.

O God, have mercy on me, a sinner.

Have pity on me, O Lord, as you pitied the tax-collector: I cry out to you, O Lord: have mercy on me! O Answerer of the pleadings of those who ask him, O Opener of his door to those who knock on it: open to me, O Lord, the door of your mercy, and grant me forgiveness for my faults, for their memory terrifies me. Indeed I know and remember my iniquities, and I cannot be purified without your mercies. May you grant me cleansing, in your grace, from the foulness of the sins that have defiled me. O compassionate Savior, O Lord of all, glory to you!

Motivation

Christ makes it clear in the Sermon on the Mount that our motivation for our actions is observed and judged by God: when we give alms, pray or fast, we are not to do it in order to show off to others, for in that case "we have received our reward." Our interior intention makes a difference to God. But this truth can be twisted, like so many truths, into something negative, something dark that the devil may use to trap us. We can begin making excuses for ourselves: "I shouldn't go to church, because if I do I'll be doing it for the wrong reason," "I don't want to turn to God or repent of my sins, because if I do it will be out of fear of hell and not out of love for him," etc. There is practically nothing we can refuse to do on this ground.

This is, obviously, a corruption of Christ's words. He said that *when* we give alms or pray or fast, that we should do it with the right intention. He was assuming that we DO these things. He never said NOT to do them, or to stop doing them, for any reason whatever. The actions themselves are good, no matter what our motivation, and it is better to do them than not to do them; Christ simply pointed out that it is best to do them for the right reasons.

Many times beginning with the wrong motivation can lead us down a path of conversion, where our intention becomes pure in the process. God can use even an imperfect intention for our spiritual benefit. In the nineteenth chapter of Luke, we have the account of a tax collector of short stature named Zacchaeus. It appears that his interest in seeing Jesus as he passed by was initially only curiosity, but Christ, pitying the poor sinner, used even this imperfect motivation to bring about a conversion of heart. Before Zacchaeus knew it, he had promised half of his possessions to the poor.

Running

The Gospel says that Zacchaeus "ran ahead" of the crowd and climbed a tree in order to see his Lord. What a virtuous run! How often is it that we run ahead of the crowd, away from the Lord, not in order to see him but in order to avoid him? We are afraid, oftentimes, both of seeing him and of being seen by him.

Here our awareness of our guilt outweighs even our curiosity to see and to know this marvelous Messiah, and we avoid him at all costs. How sad it is to see a soul which is running from God! What a dark life which hides from the Light of the world! How starved and depraved do these souls become after a lifetime of running from the God who is in every place? The Psalmist cries out at one point, "Where can I hide from your spirit? Where can I flee from your face? If I climb to the heavens, you are there; if I lie down in Sheol, you are there. If I fly with the wings of the dawn and alight beyond the sea, even there your hand would guide me, your right hand hold me fast!" (Ps 139:7-10)

This all goes to show how painful it is to be aware of sin, how deep is the wound of guilt. Even more so, this shows how crafty the devil can be, since he is the one who darkens our minds to the point where we run with all our might away from the only Doctor who can truly heal our wounds. But run as we will, our Lord is always there, waiting only for his chance, for the moment we allow him in.

Contrast

What is it about Christ that makes it tempting to run away from him in our guilt? Why is it so much more painful to recall our sins in his light, and to be in his presence in our guilt? The answer is quite simple: he shows us who we truly are, and does not allow us to lie to ourselves any longer. By ourselves, we can very skillfully hide our sins in the shadowy corners of our soul, but when we come face to face with the Light, every shadow disappears and every speck of dust becomes visible. In other words, Christ shows us our guilt by his perfect innocence; he shows us our deceit by his honesty; he shows us how filthy we are by reminding us how pure we should be.

But it does not end there, with the shocking awareness of how far we have fallen. No, the Messiah came precisely to save us who are lost, to heal us who are sick, and to wash us who are dirty. It is never too late, it is never wrong, to turn to him, even with the "mixed motivation" of desperation or fear. Our kind Lord is always waiting, always ready to purify us of our sins:

Pity me, O Lord, as you pitied the tax-collector; I cry out to you, O Lord: have mercy on me! O Answerer of the pleadings of those who ask him, O Opener of his door to those who knock on it: open to me, O Lord, the door of your mercy, and grant me forgiveness for my faults, for their memory terrifies me. Indeed I know and remember my iniquities, and I cannot be purified without your mercies. May you grant me cleansing, in your grace, from the foulness of the sins that have defiled me. O compassionate Savior, O Lord of all, glory to you!

The Fourth Sunday of Repentance

O Lord, your servants will confess you.
Regarding your grace and your truth.

Rational mouths confess you, O Good One who orders creatures, and who placed a boundary for the day, and whose word does not pass away. For when the day's work is completed and it has fulfilled its operation, it rests in its weariness, in a temporal sleep, and in its dusk it binds for us a figure of death and burial. And in its dawn, it awakens the sleeping from their sleep, as it preaches to us about our resurrection and renewal.

Noticing

The fable called "The Princess and the Pea" by Hans Christian Andersen relates how a queen, desiring to know if a certain woman was a "true princess," placed a pea underneath twenty mattresses and twenty featherbeds to see if the woman would be able to feel it when she slept on it. The delicacy of her skin, which proved itself that night, proved that she was true royalty. She was able to feel in a highly refined way; she was able to perceive something hardly perceptible, and in this she set herself apart.

211

Those who are colorblind are unable to distinguish between certain colors or shades; those who are tone deaf are unable to hear notes with precision. The senses, in other words, come in various degrees in the variety of the human race. How much more, then, within nature as a whole: we know that dogs have an extremely refined sense of smell, for example, especially those bred as "bloodhounds;" we know that many animals, especially bats, are able to sense pitches of sound completely beyond the human range; and the sight of the eagle is something almost mythical in its power.

The Creator makes nothing meaninglessly. The connection between the thing seen and the seer is an intentional one; in a real sense, God made the object so that it could be seen. Such is his goodness and love: he gives us sight as well as beauty to see, hearing as well as music to hear, and so on with all the senses. All things are meaningful and overflowing with meaning, and all things are connected to each other in this way.

DNA

Knowing this, we can in fact work "backwards" from nature and perhaps even guess the intention of the Creator: we can look at a reality in the world and ask for whose benefit it was made. We might not always have an answer, but asking in humility and reverence will only bring us closer to our Maker.

Perhaps the largest question we can ask, therefore, is regarding the ordering of the whole world. Why was the whole universe made with such an interrelating structure? For whose benefit is it so? What creature is able to perceive this order and enjoy it? The answer, in the physical world, is man alone. Only the human being, of all creatures, is able to perceive and appreciate the order of the universe. Other animals can sense particular things, desire them and even enjoy them, but only man can sense all things as a unified, interrelated whole. For the ancients, the mind and the thing it knows somehow become one and the same, which allows Aristotle to say boldly that "in a sense the soul is all existing things." (*De Anima* 3.8) In other words, we and the world are intimately interconnected, because, in the Christian perception of things, the world was made for us to enjoy and rule over: "be fruitful and multiply; fill the earth and subdue it." (Genesis 1:28) Somehow, the world is in our DNA.

The Basilica Hymn for this Sunday reflects on the world as teaching us something about ourselves, not simply as natural beings, but as beings beyond nature and beyond death, the final mark of natural things. The hymn shows how the motion of the day from light into darkness, and again into light, symbolizes our own death and resurrection:

Rational mouths confess you, O Good One who orders creatures, and who placed a boundary for the day, and whose word does not pass away. For when the day's work is completed and it has fulfilled its operation, it

rests in its weariness, in a temporal sleep, and in its dusk it binds for us a figure of death and burial. And in its dawn, it awakens the sleeping from their sleep, as it preaches to us about our resurrection and renewal.

The Fifth Sunday of Repentance

O Lord, you are a dwelling-place for us unto the ages.
Fruit-bearing trees and all cedars.

A delightful dwelling was given to Adam, the father of all, but he left it through his weakness. And in the breaking of the commandment, the evil one guided him and handed him and his children over to insatiable death. But when the Creator saw that his construction had been ruined by both of them, he sent his Son and he saved it from their hands, and, instead of the inheritance of the tree, he gave him a dwelling in heaven, and treaded a path for Adam and his sons from low Sheol to that land upon which the angels do not dare to gaze out of fear. For this, let us cry out and say: Glory to your mercies, O Lord of all!

Pleasure

Due to a well-intentioned attempt to moderate the excesses of fallen human nature, the term "pleasures of the flesh" has acquired an ugly tone in theological discussion. But, as Christ says about the ugly reality of divorce, "from the beginning it was not so." (Matthew 19:8) In the beginning, we have every reason to believe that the intention of the Creator is that we should enjoy the good things of this world in their fullness because they are, in fact, "good." This adjective is in fact repeated after each day of creation in the first chapter of Genesis, and made superlative in regard to the whole of the created world: "God looked at everything he had made and he found it very good." (Genesis 1:31)

But, unfortunately, it is no longer "the beginning" and we cannot overturn all of human history by pretending that it never happened. We no longer possess that innocence we had in the Garden, and therefore are unable to enjoy the "pleasures of the flesh" in the perfect way Adam and Eve could have before the Fall. Delight is no longer simply delight; now it is a temptation to excess, to selfishness, to greed. Now it must be approached with a conscious moderation lest it destroy us in its draw, and more often than not its draw is more mighty than our moderation. This is the reality we refer to as "concupiscence."

The Basilica Hymn of the Fifth Sunday of Repentance recalls this unfortunate turn of events with both sadness for the loss and a touching longing for the days "in the beginning:"

A delightful dwelling was given to Adam, the father of all, but he left it through his weakness.

This weakness which caused Adam to forsake or abandon the "delightful dwelling," both of the Garden of Eden and also of the peace of his own soul in union with God, was unfortunately only the first of many dark elements to rear its head in his life.

A Horrible Team

Centuries before John Milton personified Death in his masterpiece "Paradise Lost," the Church of the East had become well-acquainted with it as the logical, just consequence for sin, but one which was given through the instrumentality of "the Evil one," the devil:

> **And in the breaking of the commandment, the evil one guided him and handed him and his children over to insatiable death.**

The greed and selfishness that characterized Adam during his "weak" moment, the fall, are here shared by the character of Death, "insatiable," unable to fill his appetite and quell his desire even with the countless millions numbered among the children of Adam.

The Evil one therefore taking over and becoming the guide of the human race enslaved to sin, and Death its final dwelling-place, the plan of God seemed lost completely. These two, the devil and Death, seemed victorious for that dark and ugly time.

The Happy Fault

But God does not give up so easily, nor stand idly by while his plan for the world is skewed. Effort is a human reality, as is difficulty, and neither is it a matter of effort nor of difficulty for God to overturn the devil's scheme. Even more amazing is that, in the salvation offered in Christ, an even greater good is given to us than the one we had in the Garden. The delightful dwelling of Eden becomes less than a shadow in comparison to the dwelling of heaven to which we are called by the Lord. Even the basic construction of our nature, which was ruined by the devil and which deteriorates through the work of Death, is not only restored to its original splendor, but is made so much more magnificent in the resurrected Christ:

But when the Creator saw that his construction had been ruined by both of them, he sent his Son and he saved it from their hands, and, instead of the inheritance of the tree, he gave him a dwelling in heaven, and treaded a path for Adam and his sons from low Sheol to that land upon which the angels do not dare to gaze out of fear. For this, let us cry out and say: Glory to your mercies, O Lord of all!

The Sixth Sunday of Repentance

Turn, O my soul, to your rest.

Turn from evil and do good.

Cease henceforth, O you who are hateful in her manners, and be not a trap for others. Remember that condemnation is prepared for the wicked, and for those who commit adultery and speak impiously. O you whose soul is defiled with evils: consider that tortuous world that does not pass away, to which you are inviting your soul and your body, that they may go and inherit darkness, whose fire never fades. Repent and plead from the One who is abounding in mercies, that he may forgive your wrongdoings, and you will be saved from the violence of torture; and implore God, that he may take away the weakness of your thoughts, and have mercy on you.

The Mysterious Woman

The penitential nature of the season of "Repentance" becomes quite clear at even the most cursory glance at the Basilica Hymns of the season. Sunday by Sunday, repentance from sin becomes the focus of this season more and more, as if following the order of events recorded in the Gospel: the apostles preached, and the world repented of its sin. The first Sunday discussed how little profit there is in this life; the second called to mind the end of this life and the Bridegroom locking us out of his banquet; the third discussed the terror of remembering past sins;

the fourth discussed the symbols of death and resurrection in nature; the fifth personified evil and death as twin partners, both vying for our destruction.

The Sixth Sunday of the season of Repentance summarizes the focus of the season in a manner so direct that it is at first hard to see. No more symbols are used, nor are the words polite. It is the dialogue of a person who is simply sick of himself:

Cease henceforth, O you who are hateful in her manners, and be not a trap for others. Remember that condemnation is prepared for the wicked, and for those who commit adultery and speak impiously.

The linguistic problem in this phrase, and throughout the hymn, is the use of the feminine throughout, something that does not appear in an English translation. Literally, the second phrase would be translated, "O foul-mannered woman," but this would be misleading, for this hymn does not address any particular female. The classical world gives us some hint, since in all classical languages, including Aramaic, the word for "soul" was feminine, and in Christian literature, a dialogue between a person and his soul is a common reality. But it is not so simple here.

The brilliance of the Aramaic language is in its connection of ideas: the noun "*kathawa*" (writer) means nothing more than the one who performs the verb "*kthaw*" (to write), and the word "*kthawa*" (book) means nothing more than the product of the same verb. The close connection of concepts and the subtlety of their distinction allows for directness of thought and expression, but it also brings challenges. For example, the challenge in our hymn is that the word "*nawsha*" means both "soul" and "self," and it is used in both senses in various parts of the hymn:

O you whose soul is defiled with evils: consider that tortuous world that does not pass away, to which you are inviting your soul and your body, that they may go and inherit darkness, whose fire never fades.

It is strange to discuss "the soul of a soul," but that is what appears to be happening here ("...inviting your soul..."), unless we go beyond the ordinary classical conception of the dialogue with the soul.

The Self and the Soul

The solution to our mystery, the identity of this mysterious woman, is that she is the "self" of the speaker. This "self" is the one warned not to become "a trap for others," and the others seem to be the soul and the body, both of which are invited, through sin, to the unending torture. Understood thus, the hymn becomes a tender imploring between a human being and himself:

221

Repent and plead from the One who is abounding in mercies, that he may forgive your wrongdoings, and you will be saved from the violence of torture...

Finally the mind becomes the focal point, as both the spring of thoughts and the battleground of temptation. The petition is for strength to be given on this spiritual plane, that the battle within the self may be won:

and implore God, that he may take away the weakness of your thoughts, and have mercy on you.

Seventh Sunday of Repentance

The Lord will arise and all his enemies will be scattered.
For the wicked man rots away, conceives falsehood
and gives birth to deceit.

The Enemy looks forward to the evil hardship of the end times, to casting his net to ensnare the sons of men, and with the traps he set for Adam from the beginning he schemes against his sons in the end. He will attract the world under the guise of peace, and, if possible, he will lead even the elect astray. But not only will his desire not be fulfilled, his reign will also end. Before the eyes of all creatures he will be judged with a frightful sentence by You, O Lord, who was called the Second Adam, and all those who have followed in the footsteps of the Deceiver will be confused and exposed. And even now, You condemn all those who blaspheme you. O Lord of all, glory to you!

A History

Temptation is an intensely personal reality. The devil, who wishes to trap human souls in sin, is a crafty being and strives with all his might to tempt each one of us using our individual weaknesses. If we are by nature contemplative, he may try to make us lazy. If our personality is energetic, he may tempt us to greed, to wasting that energy on material desires. Even if our tendency is to be loving, he may try to turn that love into lust or into jealousy. Temptation is in a real way handpicked for each individual, and those being tempted can have the sense that their temptation is intensely personal.

But temptation is an extremely ancient reality, and, more importantly to our theme, a universal one. Yes, the devil tempts each one of us according to his own personal weaknesses, but he wants to destroy all of us equally, or, more precisely, he wants to destroy all of us together. He began with this goal in mind, in fact, at the very beginning with Adam and Eve, and not only does he continue today, he constantly prepares for a more and more devious assault in the future:

The Enemy looks forward to the evil hardship of the end times, to casting his net to ensnare the sons of men, and with the traps he set for Adam from the beginning he schemes against his sons in the end.

The "end of days" has been a popular theme in Christian literature from the beginning, in fact even from the first book written of the New Testament, Paul's first letter to the Thessalonians. The concern there is with the "day of the Lord," (1 Thess. 5:2) on which Christ is expected to return. To the audience of Paul in the early years of the Church, this was expected to happen within their lifetime. But because Christ has patiently waited, our perception can be that the devil is given more time to work.

The Peaceful Wolf

Who would ever sin if sin were presented to them in its fullest reality? How could someone be attracted by an offer to betray God and to cause one's own destruction? Obviously, if sin is ever to be attractive, it must be disguised. Christ describes this reality in terms of "false prophets:" "beware of false prophets, who come to you in sheep's clothing, but underneath are ravenous wolves." (Matthew 7:15) We can ask our question again, then, in the Lord's terms: who would let a wolf get near them? Only those who did not know it was a wolf.

The evil one has many disguises by which he presents himself to us, both as individuals and as a society. The temptation, for example, to go to war, even unjustly, can be presented as a concern for "national security." The betrayal of the good of natural marriage can wear the costume of "equality." Even the murder of millions of children can disguise itself under the clothing of "reproductive rights." It makes no difference how ugly or ravenous the wolf is; the simplest covering can hide it if we allow ourselves to be fooled. But Christ gives us an imperative, an order, to "beware" of such things, and therefore we are held accountable if we are fooled.

The book of Revelation describes the second beast in its own characteristically creative terms: "it had two horns like a lamb's but spoke like a dragon." (Revelation 13:11) The author John continues in his description of how this beast "deceived the inhabitants of the earth" with its great signs (Revelation 13:15). Exactly how this beast fooled everyone is not given much more than a symbolic rendering here. But returning to the beginning, to 1 Thessalonians, we have a hint: "When people are saying, 'peace and security,' then sudden disaster comes upon them." (1 Thess. 5:3). Recalling the peacefulness of the lamb, this ties together the imagery of the wolf in sheep's clothing of the Gospels as well as the beast with the voice of a dragon but the horns of a lamb. It is through a false "peace" that the evil one may make his deeds attractive to the world:

He will attract the world under the guise of peace, and, if possible, he will lead even the elect astray.

Frustration

How should we react to such a monster, whose sole purpose is our destruction, but whose expertise at lying helps him deceive us into believing him? The natural reaction, perhaps, is frustration or anger. Though a hatred for sin and for evil can be a healthy thing, this frustration can also be misguided. Unfortunately, we cannot blame the devil for our sins, as Eve did to the serpent in Genesis (3:13). God does not accept this as an excuse, for it was we who sinned, who chose to do so, who allowed ourselves to be tricked by the serpent. And so our frustration is not only with the devil and with the world. Really, our frustration is in ourselves, in our own weakness and tendency to be tricked by the lies of the enemy. How many times are we going to fall?

Moreover, our frustration can be misdirected even to God himself. Perhaps we ask, even as a society, why Christ is delaying so much in returning, why he is allowing the world to fall so far, why he is allowing us to be tempted for so long. This is a lack of trust in God, and in fact it is possible that the book of Revelation was written precisely as a response to this kind of spiritual impatience. The whole point in reflecting on the end times, on the second coming of Christ, is to reaffirm that Christ is in control, and in Christ, who took on the nature of Adam, we as well:

But not only will his desire not be fulfilled, his reign will also end. Before the eyes of all creatures he will be judged with a frightful sentence by You, O Lord, who was called the Second Adam, and all those who have followed in the footsteps of the deceiver will be confused and exposed. And even now, You condemn all those who blaspheme you. O Lord of all, glory to you!

The Holy Feast of the Transfiguration

O Lord, the God of my salvation.
They have seen your paths, O God.

O Lord, when you wished, in your love, to show your kingship and the great glory of your coming to the chosen apostles Simon, James and John, you took them up with you to Mount Tabor, and their faces shone and were lit up and your clothes were like lightning with the radiance of your flesh, the spring of life; your Father cried out and confirmed your Sonship, and made your authority known. Therefore, make us worthy to delight in that same glory, and rejoice and be glad in you, as you spread over us the light of your Countenance!

Glory to the Father and to the Son and to the Holy Spirit.

O One who is marvelous in his works, and whose mysteries are revealed through his power, in all times and places, to glorious and chosen men, to the living and the dead together, prophets as well as apostles, those worthy of the mysteries of the faithful, until he comes in the open and radiates, that each man may be perceived openly in those things which were done hiddenly. Glory to that Power which was pleased and revealed his Mystery to his friends!

True Love

If love is anything more than the expulsion of a hormone into the bloodstream, if it is something real rather than illusory, then it must be something unselfish and self-giving. The one who loves, if his love is true, must wish the best things for the one whom he loves. A husband who loves his wife must want not only to make his wife somewhat happy, but as happy as possible; not only for a moment, but for as long as possible. He must want the best things for her.

It is impossible, therefore, that love should have anything deceitful within it, since a lie is something so much worse than the truth. Indeed, the truth is among the most valuable of possessions, and no true lover would be satisfied with giving his beloved anything less. This is especially the case in the Christian faith, where the Truth is not a concept but a Person. Here the Truth told is the deepest possible truth; the most valuable truth; the most intimate, self-revealing truth.

The Basilica Hymn for the Feast of the Transfiguration, the day which commemorates Christ's ascent of Mount Tabor with three of his disciples, begins by reflecting on the love of Christ toward his beloved Church:

O Lord, when you wished, in your love, to show your kingship and the great glory of your coming to the

chosen apostles Simon, James and John, you took them up with you to Mount Tabor...

The truth of Christ's kingship and glory was one, at the time, too precious even to show to all the twelve; he picked, of them, only three to take to the mountain. But through the three he reached the Twelve, and through the Twelve he reaches us with this marvelous truth.

Participation

The truth does not lose power the more it is shared, like some worldly good. On the contrary, the more people share it the more powerful it becomes for each one of them. The truth of the Faith, the truth of the divinity of Jesus Christ, is not meant to be hidden away or locked up for fear of its being stolen; it is meant to be shared, and in its sharing the Faith expands and encompasses the entire world.

What was the reality that was shared first with Simon, James and John? What was so precious that it had to begin with such a small, select group?

...and their faces were lit up and your clothes were like lightning with the radiance of your flesh, the spring of life; your Father cried out and confirmed your Sonship, and made your authority known.

Indeed, the truth is that Christ's humanity is not the whole story. Behind this simple appearance and within it dwells the Son of God himself. For this one brief moment, Christ showed who he truly was by giving the three apostles a glimpse of the radiance of his eternal Existence.

This glimpse comes down to us in the Gospels, and we share with those three blessed apostles the vision they had with their own eyes: the skin of the Lord shone so brightly that it was blinding, and even his clothing turned a dazzling white. In our hymn, the brightness of the clothing was a result of the radiance of Christ's skin, which leads us to a deeper insight and a deeper sharing with Simon, James and John: the same Flesh which shone, which our hymn calls the "Spring of Life," is the very Flesh we consume in the Eucharist at Holy Communion. Much less than being a historical event lost in the past, the Transfiguration becomes a current mystical reality for each one of us, and a sign of the glory we hope for in our own future. Indeed, as we share in the Flesh of Christ which shone so brightly on that day, we hope to share even in his radiance:

Therefore, make us worthy to delight in that same glory, and rejoice and be glad in you, as you spread over us the light of your Countenance!

Showing What Was Hidden

St. John describes the future in careful terms in his first letter: "Beloved, we are God's children now; what we shall be has not yet been revealed. We do know that when it is revealed, we shall be like him, for we shall see him as he is." (1 John 3:2) There is still something hidden of God, as there must be in this world, for St. Paul says describes God as the one whom "no one has seen nor can see." (1 Timothy 6:16)

This hiddenness is to come to an end, however, in the vision of God we shall have in heaven. The Transfiguration, therefore, is also a peek into heaven itself, where all will be revealed:

O One who is marvelous in his works, and whose mysteries are revealed through his power, in all times and places, to glorious and chosen men, to the living and the dead together, prophets as well as apostles, those worthy of the mysteries of the faithful, until he comes in the open and radiates, that each man may be perceived openly in those things which were done hiddenly. Glory to that Power which was pleased and revealed his Mystery to his friends!

The Feast of the Assumption

Protect me from the wickedness of the evil one.

I will desire your goodness.

O mother clothed with light, plead for mercies, on the day of
your Assumption, from that Fruit which dawned from your
womb, for the assembly that has come to your banquet and
extols on the day of your passing, that in unity and perfect
love, it may magnify your name and say: blessed are you, O
woman filled with integrity; blessed are you, O young
woman, O spring of modesty; blessed are you, O Virgin and
Lady of Virgins; blessed are you, O young girl, in whom all
women are emulated and blessed; blessed are you, who, on
the day of her assumption, caused a commotion among
angels: they came and accompanied your soul in reverence
with your resplendent body; blessed are you who assembled
the apostles from every corner, and invited them to your
delightful banquet. Blessed is Christ who honored you, O
spring of purity, and brought your soul and your splendidly-
clothed body to the land of life and the bedchamber of
happiness. Ask him on our behalf for mercies and the
forgiveness of debts, that we may be worthy, with you and
with the angels, to cry out and say: halleluiah!

Glory to the Father and to the Son and to the Holy Spirit.

O Virgin, O holy daughter of David, filled with modesty and
dignity: offer pleadings and supplications on behalf of our

assembly to the Lord who chose you, that we may be made worthy of the kingdom.

A Multitude of Roles

After Adam, every man who has walked on this earth has had a mother. The mysterious, fertile concept of motherhood is therefore inescapable; every human being, in his very blood, yearns for the love of a mother, and longs to understand what it is. But some ideas are too deep to be plunged, and somehow too basic to be understood. I doubt even that mothers understand themselves and their own importance role perfectly. There is such a simple beginning to this concept of motherhood: care. But the way it expands and takes flesh is almost erratic in its variety: a mother is a nurse, a housekeeper, a cook, an engineer, an inventor, a teacher, a disciplinarian, a comforter, and much more. Such is the role of an earthly mother, and her mystery is not one to be taken lightly.

What then are we to make of spiritual motherhood? On the cross, the Lord gave two final assignments to two of his followers: to his beloved disciple, he gave the assignment to be a son to the Virgin Mary; to his mother, he gave the assignment to be the mother of his beloved. She did not give him birth, but she was to be his mother, and in him, the mother of us all, for we are all the beloved disciple of Christ. If the reality of earthly motherhood is beyond our grasp, how can we even begin to understand the spiritual motherhood of our Lady? If an earthly mother is so precious, how much more precious is she who gives birth not to our bodies, but to Christ himself within our souls? The British Jesuit poet G.M. Hopkins writes, in his poem "The Blessed Virgin Compared to the Air We Breathe," of Christ and our Lady:

> Of her flesh he took flesh:
> He does take fresh and fresh,
> Though much the mystery how,
> Not flesh but spirit now
> And makes, O marvelous!
> New Nazareth's in us,
> Where she shall yet conceive
> Him, morning, noon, and eve;
> New Bethlehem's, and he born
> There, evening, noon, and morn—
> Bethlehem or Nazareth,
> Men here may draw like breath
> More Christ and baffle death;
> Who, born so, comes to be
> New self and nobler me
> In each one and each one
> More makes, when all is done,
> Both God's and Mary's Son.

Because Mary is Christ's mother, and he is mystically born within the souls of his saints, it is Mary who continues to conceive and bear him spiritually even within our souls. There is no separation in Christ: the Christ born in Bethlehem and the Christ born in our souls is the same Son of Mary.

The Basilica Hymn for the Feast of the Assumption attempts to enumerate the roles given by Christ to our Lady, with some success. It begins with an introduction to its theme:

O mother clothed with light, plead for mercies, on the day of your Assumption, from that Fruit which dawned from your womb, for the assembly that has come to your banquet and extols on the day of your passing, that in unity and perfect love, it may magnify your name and say:

blessed are you, O woman filled with integrity;
blessed are you, O young woman, O spring of modesty;
blessed are you, O Virgin and Lady of Virgins;
blessed are you, O young girl, in whom all women are emulated and blessed;
blessed are you, who, on the day of her assumption, caused a commotion among angels: they came and accompanied your soul in reverence with your resplendent body;
blessed are you who assembled the apostles from every corner, and invited them to your delightful banquet.

This "litany" of names and roles given to our Lady praises her in increasing tones: she is "filled with integrity;" and being filled thus, she overflows as a "spring of modesty," just as all of those who believe in Christ have "living waters" flowing out of their hearts (John 7:38); even so, as a fruitful virgin, she is the "Lady of Virgins," allowing virgins on earth who consecrate themselves to the Lord to share in her work of spiritual motherhood; and despite being a young girl when she conceived the Lord, she is a model for all women, young and old.

Two beautiful images given at the end of this litany complement one another. First there is the image of the "commotion of the angels" who marveled to see body and soul of Mary enter heaven. Secondly, there is a reference to a touching episode in eastern Marian hagiography, in which our Lady, laying on her deathbed, asks to see the apostles one last time before her dormition. How sweet must have been the love between the Lord's mother and his dearest friends! And so, responding to this love, the apostles assemble "from every corner" to bid their earthly farewell to the mother of their Messiah.

The Point of This All

Our Lady is many things, but her ultimate role is to be a pointer to Christ her son, and every authentic devotion to Mary must lead directly to Jesus himself. So is the case with the spirituality of the Church of the East and of our hymn, which returns to the point, the meaning of the whole universe and of salvation history, the Messiah:

> **Blessed is Christ who honored you, O spring of purity, and brought your soul and your splendidly-clothed body to the land of life and the bedchamber of happiness. Ask him on our behalf for mercies and the forgiveness of debts, that we may be worthy, with you and with the angels, to cry out and say: halleluiah!**
>
> *Glory to the Father and to the Son and to the Holy Spirit.*
>
> **O Virgin, O holy daughter of David, filled with modesty and dignity: offer pleadings and supplications on behalf of our assembly to the Lord who chose you, that we may be made worthy of the kingdom.**

The Feast of the Adorable Cross

The Lord rules over the nations.

The Lord rules forever.

May your cross rule in heaven, may your cross rule on earth, and may your cross crown the assemblies who confess your cross.

In heaven and on earth.

May the cross which was seen in heaven, and revealed in mercies to the earthly, exalt our miserable race, and enter its establisher into heaven.

Your adornment and your glory; your glory is victorious.

The cross was victorious, the cross is victorious, the cross defeated Satan, and shamed the wall of crucifiers, and gladdened the assembly of his adorers.

Its rays lighten the world.

The cross of light that was shown to Constantine in heaven went to war like a mighty soldier at the head of his hosts.

From a people without mercy.

May your cross, O Lord, which was obscured due to the evil of the crucifiers let its rays fly over creation and enlighten the world to its ends.

It will abolish wars to the ends of the earth.

May the cross which reigns in the heights give peace to the lowest depths, for height does not need peace: pacify, O Lord, mankind.

That he may show his greatness.

The cross gave victory to our nature, the cross lifted up our poverty; the cross exalted our insignificance, and entered its placement in heaven.

The world and all its inhabitants.

By your cross, may all be reconciled, and by your cross may all be renewed, and by your cross, O Lord, guard us from the wiles of the deceiver.

May your blessing be upon your people.

Through your cross, O Lord, may priests and kings, your propitiators, be reconciled, and through your cross may your Church rejoice, O her exalter through your abasement.

We your people and the sheep of your flock.

By your cross, O Lord, may the world which is shaken by wars be pacified, and by your command, may the sword which lays waste to our dwelling be abolished.

The Lord will show his salvation.

Through your cross was salvation for the nations who believed in your cross; and by your cross was also condemnation for the nations who denied your cross.

It will be like the tree planted by a stream of water.

The holy cross resembles the spring that flowed in Eden, and the wise drank from it and even the ignorant gained clarity.

Its branches are as great as a handsome brightness.

The holy cross resembles the tree of life in the Church, whose fruits are suitable for eating, and whose leaves are fitting for healing.

Glory to the Father, to the Son and to the Holy Spirit.

May your cross rule in heaven, may your cross rule on earth,

and may your cross crown the assemblies who

confess your cross.

From age to age, amen, amen.

Holy One, Holy Mighty One, Holy Immortal One:

have mercy on us.

Church & State

A great deal of harm has been done by oversimplifying the relationship between political authority and the truth of the Christian faith. A glaring example of this is the intermingling of political and Church leadership that has occurred in the West at various times throughout the centuries, where bishops and princes became hard to distinguish, and even went to war with each other – the "Papal States" being a pure symbol of this unhappy commingling. This form of mixing the spiritual power of the Church and the physical power of the State ended up dividing and embittering the State and corrupting and defiling the Church.

On the other hand, for an individual in power to completely ignore his faith, or for a nation to "put its faith aside" when it comes to politics, is divisive and corruptive not only of a country but even of an individual soul. To believe and be convinced, for example, that a human life is incalculably precious, and then, when it comes to "politics," to ignore that conviction, is to divide the conscience, to tear the heart into pieces. It is also to tear the mind into pieces: naturally, if something is true it is true; if it is a fact in Church, it is a fact everywhere else. A life is a life equally during a Sunday sermon, when it comes to the question of a country going to war, and when it comes to the legality of abortion. To split the mind and the conscience is to do damage to the deepest part of the human being, and to do this is contrary to the very nature of the State.

The goal of government, in all classical thinking, Christian and non-Christian, is to encourage its citizens to become good people. Asking them to deny their consciences, or to put them aside, or to split their beliefs into separated modules, is to commit a crime directly against this goal. When a nation does this, it causes division and war within the souls of its citizens, while its main purpose is to bring about virtue, honesty and peace.

It is this peace within the heart of man that is the first goal both of Christianity and of the State, each in its own way. From the part of the State, this peace is brought about by laws which encourage selflessness and love, bringing about peace both in society and within the individual. From the part of the Faith, a higher, truer peace is provided in which Christ himself, described as the "Peace of the World" in the Chaldean Liturgy, comes to dwell within the soul of the believer. The Church and the State have the same goal, and while they should not overlap one another, it is wise that they should work together.

Whether the Christianization of the Roman Empire in the early fourth century was ultimately a good thing or a bad thing, both for the Church and for the State, is a difficult thing to gauge, even for the most seasoned historian. Certainly, there was an increase in the number of believers, but how authentic this faith was if it was forced upon the individual by the State, or given substantial material benefit, is something visible only to God; certainly, there was a spreading of Christian values, but how seriously the Emperors of Rome lived these values is likewise lost to our judgment. The celebration of the Feast of the Cross is, in its first conception, a celebration of the "Cross of Light" seen by Constantine which led him to victory and to the Christian faith, and to the subsequent finding of the actual wood of the cross of Christ by his mother Helen. As such, it is the celebration of an idealized relationship between Church and State, whether or not this relationship ever existed in reality. Today is a celebration of the peace brought about by the cross of Christ, both in the soul and in society.

An Ancient Reality

The book of Genesis recounts the inspired understanding of God's first thoughts when creating the world. The power of its images, therefore, is a real one, because every detail in them is intended to have significance "from the foundation of the world," that is, to the most mysterious depths of human life on this earth. It is no wonder, then, that the hymns sung on the Feast of the Cross make so many references to the account of creation in the book of Genesis, and other accounts of the "earliest days," the days when everything became what it is. This is because the crucifixion of the Savior of the world must be the "crux" of all of history; it cannot be otherwise. The cross, in other words, is the fulfillment of all that ever happened before it, and the guiding light of all that occurred after it.

Because the cross of Christ reaches so deeply into human history, down to its very blueprint, we believers are free to make creative parallels between it and the primordial images of the books of Genesis and Exodus:

The holy cross resembles the spring that flowed in Eden, and the wise drank from it and even the ignorant gained clarity.

The holy cross resembles the tree of life in the Church, whose fruits are suitable for eating, and whose leaves are fit for healing.

The cross of our Life-Giver resembles that which Moses lifted up in the desert: that one gave life to the Hebrews, this one to the four corners.

Even deeper are natural symbols, such as the dawning of the sun:

The holy cross resembles the sun which dawns in the firmament, whose rays fly through the air, and whose light gladdens creatures.

Finally, images are brought even from the New Testament and from heaven itself to help express the meaning of this particular piece of wood:

The holy cross resembles a flawless pearl, which head merchants bought and through which became wealthy and exalted.

The assembly of the faithful, when it stands in the churches, resembles the assembly of angels who extol the Divine dwelling.

A Great Light

This all goes to say that the Christian Faith makes an enormous difference in human life. It is not a matter of opinion or of picking a favorite religion. It is a matter of true and false, of right and wrong, of light and darkness, and the cross is the ultimate catalyst of this transition of humanity from darkness to light:

We are not ashamed of your cross, O Jesus the victorious King, for in it you saved our nature from slavery to sin.

O cross, whose authority extends above in heaven and blow on earth: may your peace rule over the Church, that she may sing praise to you every day.

The gorgeous beauty of the cross radiates across the whole world, and the heavenly and the earthy gain true hope.

O cross which is filled with mercies from your procession to your paths: you see creatures shaken and come to pacify them.

The First Sunday of the Cross

Out of the depths I cried to you, O Lord, and you heard my voice
I meditated at night, and I meditated in my heart; I meditated and
my spirit was shaken.

I have been considering your judgment seat, O Christ, and all my limbs have been shaking in fear. Who will be my help before your judgment seat who is from my race - from humanity? All my friends and dear ones will stand and look upon me from far away. O Just Judge, according to the greatness of your mercy, have pity on me, O Compassionate One, and not, O Lord, according to the many debts I have incurred.

Glory to the Father and to the Son and to the Holy Spirit.

We are not ashamed, O Lord, of your cross, because of the great power hidden within it. If pagans and Jews mock your preaching, they cannot ever eradicate the truth. Lo, both of them together cry out for your righteousness: the Jews are scattered, and the teaching of the pagans is abolished. Behold, they witness together that great, O Lord, is your power!

Injustice

Of all the flaws of human nature, the most tragic has been the tendency to believe a lie. It was this flaw that made us subject to the first temptation in the garden. Not that that first temptation began as an outright lie – it began as a doubt, with the serpent asking Eve, "did God really tell you not to eat of any of the trees of the garden?" This conversation began with a simple question, but ended with a lie – "You certainly will not die!" (Genesis 3:4). And because Eve believed that lie and Adam stood by silently and watched it all happen, sin entered the world, along with suffering and injustice, and all the evils we see around us today. The destruction of the human race began with one little lie, and it took nothing less that Truth incarnate dying on the cross to undo the damage wrought by that little lie.

But that first lie was not, unfortunately, the last. Every lie, large or small, continues the destruction and the suffering caused by that first lie. Damage can be done by even a "white lie" – both to the one telling the lie and to the one believing it. The fact is that, excepting extraordinary circumstances, the truth should be told when and where it is owed, and nothing else. It is only fair to do so, and it is unfair, it is unjust, criminal, to deceive.

The darkest injustice can be presented to an individual soul when, for example, one is told that hell does not exist. Such a "small" lie! Such a lie that can be told with such a pleasant intention – to save someone from worry or sorrow, or fear! But the damage that can be done, the spiritual crime committed by telling or believing this lie, is deep indeed. It can take many forms: "you are a good person, I'm sure you're going to heaven;" "God wouldn't punish someone in that way, he is a God of love;" etc. Such phrases are rattled off with the greatest confidence, as if we are the ones to judge souls, or as if it is our job to tell God what mercy means. It is no friend who tells us such things, and neither are we being friends to others when we do so.

Fear of the Lord

If it is possible for a merely human friendship to be ruined by miscommunication or misunderstanding, all the more is this the case with our relationship with God – not that he miscommunicates or misunderstands, but that we do. If our love of God is to grow, it must begin rightly, with the right understanding and the right mode of communication. For example, if we understand God as simply vengeful and angry all the time, with no sense of compassion or mercy, our natural reaction would be to run away, to avoid such a frightening persona, and therefore there would be no communication between us and God, and no friendship. But if, on the other hand, our understanding of God is beneath him, if we envision him as "just a buddy" and ignore the fact that he is also the Creator of the universe, our picture is entirely wrong and we are communicating, in this buddy-buddy way, not with God but with an idol that we have made for ourselves.

This being the case, it must be true to say that having a picture of God that makes him out to be nothing more than a "nice guy" actually pushes us farther away from him, even if the intention is otherwise. Even if, in other words, we paint a pleasant picture of God so that we or others may feel more comfortable and come closer to it, we are in fact only coming closer to a picture, and not to the true God.

But this is not simply the case of an objective fact on the one hand and idolatry on the other. The objective fact of God's justice and punishment of sinners is not only a reality that we must come to terms with if we are to be realistic; human psychology is such that knowing and realizing this fact allows us to come closer to him. If God is merely merciful, we may ignore him until he is needed. But if he is also perfectly just, then he cannot be ignored, then for our own sake we must strive to make him more and more a part of our lives.

Christ came precisely for this, in fact: for the Just God to show his mercy as well, not so that his justice is put aside, but to make known how he wishes to live among us and within us. Another way to say this is this: in recollecting God's judgment, we cling so much more closely to Christ, who is our compassionate and loving Mediator with the Father. If there were no judgment, this motivation to cling to Christ would no longer exist.

The True Friend

This is how a balanced meditation on God's judgment can and must bring us only closer to a true, deep friendship with the Messiah. As any true friend, Christ speaks us the truth even if it is hard to hear, he challenges us always to strive more and more to perfection rather than diluting us with empty compliments to build up our "self-esteem," and he shows us our weakness so that we turn more and more to him for strength, rather than assuring us of our own goodness and putting aside God's expectations for our lives. The Master is expecting a large return from his vineyard when he comes back. Only a false friend would give us false comfort by telling us of the Master's compassion; the true Friend, Christ, reminds us constantly to work and to repent. It is this true Friend who will be standing alongside us on the day of judgment; the others will only stand afar off and stare:

I have been considering your judgment seat, O Christ, and all my limbs have been shaking in fear. Who will be my help before your judgment seat who is from my race - from humanity? All my friends and dear ones will stand and look upon me from far away. O Just Judge, according to the greatness of your mercy, have pity on me, O Compassionate One, and not, O Lord, according to the many debts I have incurred.

The Second Sunday of the Cross

In it our heart is glad.

The holy Church extols your holy cross, O Savior, in which creation was freed from error, and preaches its victory with the assemblies of her children. And because daughter Zion lost her case through it, the Church has victory through its power, and boasts in its name, as she pleads from you to guard her from injuries.

I said "I will guard my path and not sin with my lips."

The desires of the passing world have separated me from you, and through them the rebel sets traps for me and ensnares me, that I may not please you, O Lord. And as I earned little, and the world and its enticements passed away, regrets and sufferings overcame me. For I see that the hope of my life has passed away, and now I have no refuge besides you, O Lord. In the greatness of your mercies, turn to me, and in your grace, have pity on me; rescue me from my sins, as is your way, O Lover of mankind! O Lord, forgive me!

Investment

In his unsurpassable mercies, God created us with many natural gifts and talents, and second only to the intellect, the greatest gift he gave us at our creation was the gift of free will. Though all things are in his hands, God deigned to allow some things to be in ours, and he respects that freedom until today; that is, he does not force our will to any decision, but in his grace he guides us gently to the truth and goodness that come from him. What is in our hands, then, is ultimately the following: to decide what to do with the gifts God has given us. The Master in Matthew 25 who gives a different amount of coins to his three servants expects them back with 100% increase, but not all of them live up to this expectation.

It is easy to call ourselves "servants of God," and in fact giving ourselves this name is Christ's direct command: "When you have done all that you have been commanded, *say to yourselves*, 'We are unprofitable servants; we have done only what was our duty.'" (Luke 17:10). But this servanthood toward God is not simply a matter of names. Do we act as servants, unprofitable or otherwise, or do we rebel in disobedience to our Master? Do we follow other masters, like money or pleasure? Do we run away from our true and kind Master only to find ourselves enslaved to another? Indeed, the temptation to follow, and ultimately serve, the pleasures of this world is a real one:

The desires of the passing world have separated me from you, and through them the rebel sets traps for me and ensnares me, that I may not please you, O Lord.

Starvation

The parable of the two sons in Luke 15 gives the example of the son who ran away from his father after taking half of his father's property. Having "squandered it on a life of dissipation," he finds himself in servitude to another master, one who does not even provide him with the basic essentials of life, for "he longed to feast on the pods on which the swine fed." The "prodigal son" turns back to his father after realizing his own hunger.

What hunger it must have taken to make this son, who had insulted his father so badly, return to him in shame! But what of us? What type of spiritual starvation must come upon us before we return to our Father above, after we have spent our gifts and our life running after the passing and empty pleasures of this world? How dark is that moment when, having sold our soul and filled ourselves with some sinful delight, we realize that it no longer tastes as it did! How shockingly sad when we discover we have been duped by a lying salesman! Indeed, all the delights of this world, delicious as they are, without God are fading in flavor rapidly, and in the end leave us starving even for our basic sustenance of life:

And as I earned little, and the world and its enticements passed away, regrets and sufferings overcame me, for I saw that the hope of my life has passed away...

Crawling Back

The first and worst mistake we can make in thinking about God is in reducing him to our mindset, in "creating him in our image." This mode of idolatry is expressed when we fear his anger and avoid returning to him. Yes, God is perfectly just, but his mercy is perfect as well, and, according to Christ's own symbol, he is a Father who enthusiastically runs out to greet us when we turn back to him, no matter what we have squandered our life upon. Our return to him is humbling indeed, but this humility only puts us in our place in relation to God. Indeed, even the fear we have of God's punishment should be motivation to turn back to him. Between the spiritual starvation, the promise of mercy, and the threat of punishment, there are many ropes in the net which pulls us back to the Father:

...and now I have no refuge besides you, O Lord. In the greatness of your mercies, turn to me, and in your grace, have pity on me; rescue me from my sins, as is your way, O Lover of mankind! O Lord, forgive me!

The Third Sunday of the Cross

I will exalt you, O Lord my King.

Who walked in darkness.

Before your crucifixion, O Savior, the deceit of Satan had troubled the whole creation, and until then the race of men had been enslaved under the yoke of Death, the murderer of our race. But the wood of the Cross killed Death and undid Sin, and raised our race from the dead. The exalted beings marveled at our race which had been raised and brought above all sufferings. Because of this, we cry out unceasingly and say: glory to you who raised up our race!

In it our heart is glad.

In the hour the wood of the Cross was set up, you shook the foundations of death, O Lord. And those whom Sheol had swallowed up in their sins and left shaking, in terror, your command restored to life, O Lord. Because of this, we also glorify you: O Christ the King, have mercy on us!

The Old Days

It is a deep element in human nature to long for a near-forgotten past, when "things were better." This is not simply the grumbling of the older generation of today, a lament against the young who "have no respect" and a world which is "not like it used to be." This is truly a desire for Eden, a wish for things to return to that primordial past when there was neither sin nor suffering. This is not to say that every age is equal, or that "things" are not actually worse now than they were a generation ago. But whether this is true or not (and it would take a mighty intellect indeed to be able to perceive and gauge every element of an entire generation, much less two), the complaint would still exist. Even if things are better now than they were before, a part of us would still gaze at the past with wistful eyes. This is both because, in addition to the deep and almost subconscious awareness of the loss of Eden, for better or for worse, the past was experienced in the freshness of youth, and the present, for better or for worse, is being experienced in the bitterness of older age.

This is the case of a fallen and broken humanity. But the reality of grace dramatically changes this, even causing a complete reversal. In the light of the Fall, the past was a beautiful time without pain; but in the light of the cross of Christ and the abundant graces showered upon us through it, there is no better time than the present. Thus the Basilica Hymn of this Sunday looks back toward the past with critical eyes:

Before your crucifixion, O Savior, the deceit of Satan had troubled the whole creation, and until then the race of men had been enslaved under the yoke of Death, the murderer of our race.

The Revolt

Similarly, the ordinary way of thinking about the "status quo," the way things currently are, is that authority is good and disobedience is bad. While this is obviously the case in the ultimate sense of things, there is a way in which even this basic ordering is reversed by the cross. When the authority, when the one being obeyed, is invalid, then obviously rebellion is the right path; when the one giving orders is Satan, then the best thing we can be is disobedient.

This is not merely imaginative thinking. Satan is named the "prince of this world," (John 12:31) and Paul refers to the "reign of darkness" (Col 1:13). This prince, this reign, is false and misleading. They are governments which are invalid, and which deserve rebellion and disobedience, because they themselves are in fact nothing more than rebellions against the King of Kings and Lord of Lords. Because of the nature of the world today, there are times when we must choose between obedience to a worldly authority and obedience to God. Christ chose obedience to God, and by his rebellion against the evil reign of Satan through his death on the cross, he single-handedly overturned the authority that had enslaved this world:

But the wood of the cross killed Death and undid Sin, and raised our race from the dead.

On Earth, as it is in Heaven

Finally, the dividing line between heaven and earth being precisely this difference in kingship, Christ made peace and unified the two parts of creation which had been sundered by the disobedience of Adam. In Christ, in his death on the cross, which was the ultimate act of obedience to the Father, making up for the disobedience of Adam, and the ultimate act of selfless love, making up for the selfishness of Adam, earth, meaning the souls of the faithful, the Church, becomes like heaven in obeying the will of the Father. In Christ, we become a new kingdom, one which has risen up by grace to defeat the reign of the evil one and established, in the holy Church and in our souls, the new kingship of the Messiah and the new obedience to the will of the Father.

Because of this, the joy known on earth is felt in heaven among the angels – for if Christ said that there will be joy in heaven over one sinner who repents (Luke 15:4), how much more will the angels rejoice over the whole Church, the segment of the human race which rose up against Satan in Christ and accepted the Kingdom of the Father:

The exalted beings marveled at our race which had been raised and brought above all sufferings. Because of this, we cry out unceasingly and say: glory to you who raised up our race!

The Fourth Sunday of the Cross

The heavens make known the glory of God.
O the depth of the richness and the wisdom of
the knowledge of God!

The mouth of creatures is unable to relate the greatness of your Wisdom, O Great Unlimited Sea, for the things of heaven and earth, with their adornments, are unable to teach us of your Greatness. But, through our wretched nature, you have brought us near to your knowledge, and through the shame and contempt of the Cross, you have made creation into a true Body without corruption for yourself, you who are the Head who pours forth blessings and new life in the kingdom of heaven. Therefore, we all cry out and say: thanksgiving be to the mercies that had pity on our nature!

For the honor of your Name.

We revere the memory of your adorable passion, O Savior, and also your Cross, whose joyful feast is prepared for us in love, in which we all receive forgiveness of sins and faults, and in which new life apart from Sheol arises, to the defeat of the Jews, the boast of your faithful Church, and the glory of your victorious unlimited Power.

Immeasurable in Miles

When we are stuck with something seemingly impossible, our two options are to do the best we can or give up entirely.

Depending on the situation, either one of these options could be the right thing to do. But what if something is not "seemingly" impossible, but actually impossible? Is that a clear sign that we should give up, or can we still try our best, knowing for certain that we can never reach our goal? And what would be the point of such a futile exercise?

It is impossible, on earth or in heaven, for a human mind to comprehend the Nature of God. On earth, it is difficult even to get a hint of God's essence, and even this hint is completely impossible without his help, his self-revelation and his grace.

If this were the whole story, we would have no problem: we could simply give up. But there is more: this near-impossible task of knowing God is the deepest drive in the human heart. It is the most important thing we can do; it is what gives meaning to our life. And so the choice is practically out of our hands: impossible though it is to comprehend God, we must try our best anyway, if our life is to find its meaning. Even if we cannot determine the very edges of the ocean and its depth, we must at least jump in and swim.

But there is more wisdom offered, and more hope than we expect. God, who gave us this desire to know him, does not abandon us to a pointless pursuit. Though on our own we have trouble even knowing that he exists (and this is evidenced by those who deny his existence), with his help we can come much nearer to our goal. The wisdom offered by the revelation of God to his people, beginning with Abraham as encapsulated by the holy Scriptures, is generally a humbling reality. That is, almost all of our talk about God is expressed in terms of un-knowing rather than knowing. For example, when we say that God is "immortal," all we are saying is that he is "not mortal." It is not a positive, solid statement that we understand; it is simply saying that God is not like we are in this particular way. The same goes for many of our terms: "infinite" only means "not finite;" "immutable" means "not changing;" etc. Even the terms we use that sound positive are really not so: "all-powerful" really only means (to us) "not weak, as we are," "holy" means "not sinful," and so on. The actual, positive meaning of these terms is something beyond our understanding entirely. In other words, we know that these words and statements are true, but we do not know what they mean. That is the humbling reality of our talk about God.

The great irony is that we are so limited in our language about God despite the fact that we have abundant evidence of his goodness. St. Paul even blames those who deny God despite everything they see around them: "For what can be known about God is evident to them, because God made it evident to them. Ever since the creation of the world, his invisible attributes of eternal power and divinity have been able to be understood and perceived in what he has made." (Romans 1:19-20). In other words, if we want to know what God is like, we can simply look at the universe, at nature, at all the things he has made, and, even if we will not find precise, scientific terminology, we will at least have some grasp of his Nature. But, again, even this grasp is minute and insufficient to describe the enormity of God's Essence:

> **The mouth of creatures is unable to relate the greatness of your Wisdom, O Great Unlimited Sea, for the things of heaven and earth, with their adornments, are unable to teach us of your Greatness.**

Know Thyself

Is there any evidence missing in this picture? And piece of the puzzle we have neglected? If in creation we have a glimpse of the goodness of the Creator, perhaps we should look to the account of creation for another hint. On the sixth day, God created cattle and other animals, and then, speaking again, he said "Let us make man in our image, after our likeness." (Genesis 1:26). If creation somehow reflects God's Nature, all the more so must man, because man is his image. But how this reflection occurs, and in what way man is God's image, is left to other hymns to explain. The Basilica Hymn of the Fifth Sunday of Elijah mentions this fact only in passing, only as a building block to another, deeper point:

> **But, through our wretched nature, you have brought us near to your knowledge...**

Recapitulation

A simple glimpse at a newspaper will affirm the adjective "wretched" used to describe human nature above, and the concurrent amazement that through this wretchedness somehow God makes himself known to us. But there is something inappropriate about this: God is in no way wretched, and so this tension within human nature between its ugly sinfulness and its splendid imaging of God's nature is unresolved when left alone. But God leaves nothing alone; he pursues and perfects till the end.

Adam, the first father of humanity, failed, and through him, the source of human nature, the head of our race, all his descendents fell with him. The imagery of "head" and "body" used in St. Paul's writings comes to the foreground in the theology of the Church of the East, where because the initial "head" of humanity (Adam) failed, the "body" (the rest of us) begins to decay. It was not until Christ, the true Image of God and the Head of the Church, came did the human race become regenerated, reborn into this new Body, with Christ as the head. The ultimate "re-capitulation," or "head replacement" occurred on the Cross, where Christ replaced Adam's disobedience by his obedience, and took his place at the Head of humanity.

The question changes, therefore. It is no longer a matter of us knowing God, but of God knowing us in Christ and as members of Christ. We had fallen away from our true Head, but Christ became one of us to rescue us from that fall, to bind us to himself as his mystical Body, and to present us to the Father as his own members. That is why St. Paul describes the turn from idolatry to the worship of the true God in terms of being known: "...but now that you have come to know God, or rather to be known by God, how can you turn back again to the weak and destitute elemental powers?" (Galatians 4:9).

Christ is the Head who gives meaning to our lives, who allows us to understand ourselves as belonging to God, and therefore to understand, in some mystical way, God himself in Christ:

> **...and through the shame and contempt of the cross, you have made creation into a true Body without corruption for yourself, you who are the Head who pours forth blessings and new life in the kingdom of heaven. Therefore, we all cry out and say: thanksgiving be to the mercies that had pity on our nature!**

The Fifth Sunday of the Cross

In it our heart is glad.

The cross was established in Jerusalem, and all creatures were gladdened; greedy death was unraveled in it, and the power of demons was taken away; it chased the Jews away to the four corners of the earth, and it gathered the nations together, and brought them into the Kingdom, that Paradise of heaven, which Adam lost when he disobeyed, the Second Adam conquered in Judah, returning its land to the Kingdom.

He seized power in heaven and on earth, for behold, assemblies of angels worship before him, and they all cry out in one voice: thanksgiving to the Son of the Lord of All!

Turn, O my soul, to your rest

O my miserable soul, when you take up your lamp, await and listen for the glorious Bridegroom and, with the wise virgins, prepare and stay awake with them, and with your eyes not hanging in sleep shout the praises of the Lord, and beg him, saying: "O God, forgive me and have mercy on me, O Lover of mankind!"

Falling Asleep

In discussing the end of time, St. Paul urges the Thessalonians, "let us not sleep as the rest do, but let us stay alert and sober. Those who sleep go to sleep at night, and those who are drunk get drunk at night. But since we are of the day, let us be sober." (1 Thessalonians 5:6-8). From the time of this (most likely) earliest-written of all pieces of Christian literature, we have a sense of the symbolic meaning of "sleep" and "wakefulness." To be "asleep" means to be unprepared for Christ's coming, in a state of forgetfulness of his existence and his presence already among us; that is, in a state of sin. Spiritual wakefulness, on the other hand, means being in a consistent state of awareness of God's existence and presence, and living as one who knows God and is near him.

"What if you died today? What would you say to God?" If this is a jarring question to us, then perhaps there is some part of our soul that is asleep. Christ himself, again in discussing the last days, uses similar imagery: "Then" (that is, "at the end") the kingdom of heaven will be like ten virgins who took their lamps and went out to meet the bridegroom...since the bridegroom was long delayed, they all became drowsy and fell asleep." (Matthew 25:1,5). The closer one examines this parable, the more confusing it becomes. On the one hand, there are five wise virgins and five foolish; at the end of the parable Christ's message is "therefore, stay awake, for you know neither the day nor the hour." (Matthew 25:13). But the problem is that all of the virgins, wise and foolish alike, fall asleep! Not even the "model" virgins, the wise ones, were able to stay awake until the coming of the bridegroom. What distinguished them was not their ability to stay awake, but their foresight in bringing extra oil for their lamps (Matthew 25:4).

We know what staying awake signifies: living a virtuous life, a life without the sleep of sin. But we are told (and rightly so) that on our own this kind of life is utterly impossible, even for the wise. Yet, with Christ's command to "stay awake," the impossible comes within our grasp, for his is the grace that allows us to love God at all, especially with all our hearts, and our neighbors as ourselves. Perhaps this love, given by Christ, is the oil that supplies light in the darkness, and envigors our drooping eyes. The Basilica Hymn of this Sunday continues the seasonal theme of the end of the world, and brings these images together:

O my miserable soul, when you take up your lamp, await and listen for the glorious Bridegroom and, with the wise virgins, prepare and stay awake with them, and with your eyes not hanging in sleep shout the praises of the Lord, and beg him, saying: "O God, forgive me and have mercy on me, O Lover of mankind!"

The Sixth Sunday of the Cross

In it, our enemies are defeated.

We have gained an unending boast against death in the Cross of Christ, and in his Resurrection from among the dead. For by his suffering, he uprooted the sentence upon us. In great, unending glory, then, we all cry out and say: Only-Begotten God the Word, who assumed our mortal body, have pity, O Lord, on your servants, who confess your cross!

May our first sins not be recalled against us.

Who does not grieve that our faults have multiplied and our iniquities increased, and that all men have drowned in the sleep of desires as in a sea? The truth has dimmed and injustice has shone in the thorn bush of our malice, and Justice has become zealous in calling us to account in the war, famine, carnage, and earthquakes that have happened. All the signs that the Lord pointed out have been fulfilled in our days, for by our sins the end of the world reaches us. Let us shed mournful tears as we say: O Lord, who created us in his grace, absolve our souls and have mercy on us!

Hurricanes, Sins and the End of the World

The calamities that have been striking the globe in past years have given rise to many discussions about the nature of such evils and their cause. Even more so have hurricanes Katrina and Wilma sparked questions in America – not because they are worse calamities than those that have struck Asia, but because they are, so to speak, in our own backyard. Indeed, it is a testimony to our self-centeredness that a single American being kidnapped or harmed hails many times more media attention than tens of thousands of non-Americans being killed. In any case, it is natural that tragedy cause reflection.

But the manner in which many so-called Christians have reflected upon these recent tragedies has been at best incautious and at worst directly contrary to the teaching of Christ. When Katrina, for example, struck and basically destroyed New Orleans, there was no shortage of preachers claiming that the hurricane was sent by God to punish the sins of the people of that city – these preachers merely pointed out the (admittedly) sinful behavior exhibited by many during Mardi Gras, and felt justified in explaining to the world why God did this. This is against the clear teaching of Christ. In the thirteenth chapter of Luke, Christ answers a nearly identical question: whether certain people were killed because of their sins. He answers very clearly: "Do you think that because these Galileans suffered in this way they were greater sinners than all other Galileans? By no means!" Not only does Christ answer "no," but it is an exclamative, loud "NO." He himself brings up another case – even closer to the tragedies we have witnessed in these past months – of a "natural disaster:" "Or those eighteen people who were killed when the tower at Siloam fell upon them – do you think they were more guilty than everyone else who lived in Jerusalem? By no means!"

This is not, however, the end of the story. Christ continues, after saying "no, these people were not killed because of their sins," to point to us all: "but if you do not repent, worse will happen to you." Christ's teaching is this: it is not our business to speculate why someone else was harmed; the sins of other people are not our concern at all; our concern is our own sins and our own repentance. To take even a single step into someone else's conscience, to spend even a moment judging another person's heart, is to disobey Christ.

A second form of speculation that these frequent natural disasters have sparked is that concerning the end of the world. This is indeed a more valid approach to understanding these events (Christ in fact tells us to read "the signs of the times"), but, like anything, it can easily become twisted and anti-Christian if we are not careful. In the twenty-fourth chapter of Matthew, Christ discusses the signs that will accompany the end of time: "Nation will rise against nation, and kingdom against kingdom; there will be famines and earthquakes from place to place. All these are the beginning of the labor pains... Many false prophets will arise and deceive many, and because of the increase

271

of evildoing, the love of many will grow cold...And this gospel of the kingdom will be preached throughout the world as a witness to all nations, and then the end will come."

Christ continues in this way to give details of the signs of the end times, but if we are to truly understand his Word we must ask what his purpose is in telling us such things: why should we be on the lookout? The answer is certainly not "to rub our special knowledge in people's faces." It is with a humble and contrite heart that we should be awaiting the coming of the Lord: "But of that day and hour no one knows, neither the angels of heaven, nor the Son, but the Father alone."

Christ not only asks us to be humble in the estimation of our own knowledge, but gives us an example of humility – he claims not to know the day and hour himself! The message is not to be arrogant with our supposed knowledge of the future, but to be weary and prepared: "Be sure of this: if the master of the house had known the hour of night when the thief was coming, he would have stayed awake and not let his house be broken into. So too, you also must be prepared, for at an hour you do not expect, the Son of Man will come."

Our own Chaldean Church reflects on the end of the world, its signs, and its connection to sin on this Sunday. It is humble and fearful, and appropriate for all of us to pray together:

Who does not grieve that our faults have multiplied and our iniquities increased, and that all men have drowned in the sleep of desires as in a sea? The truth has dimmed and injustice has shone in the thorn bush of our malice, and Justice has become zealous in calling us to account in the war, famine, carnage, and earthquakes that have happened. All the signs that the Lord pointed out have been fulfilled in our days, for by our sins the end of the world reaches us. Let us shed mournful tears as we say: O Lord, who created us in his grace, absolve our souls and have mercy on us!

The Seventh Sunday of the Cross

I will strengthen him and honor him.

You have abolished and loosened, through your holy cross, O Christ the King, all the error of idols, and you have exalted and honored all those who believe in you. For lo, the splendid Service of your hidden and holy Mysteries is extolled like a bride in honoring the martyrs who were killed for your sake. The priests who sing, and we also who glorify you, say: O Lord, may the true faith be guarded until eternity!

That are written with a pen of iron and with a diamond stylus.

Like an image engraved on a tablet, I am searched, O Lord, in my debts and sins which are written upon my skin and inscribed, and at all times shamefacedness hides my soul. O my Savior, be the absolver of my guilt, and have mercy on me.

The Hidden God

There is a real tension in theology, corresponding to a tension in reality, between understanding God as revealed and recognizing him as hidden. On the one hand, "his invisible attributes of eternal power and divinity have been understandable and perceivable in what he has made" (Romans 1:20); on the other hand, "who has known the mind of the Lord, or who has been his counselor?" (Romans 11:34). No matter how much we see of God in nature, in Scripture, and even in his fullest revelation in the flesh, in Jesus Christ, he always remains beyond our comprehension; no matter how much he reveals of himself, he still stays somehow hidden.

This eventually causes us a problem. Because we are God's image, we imitate his Nature in a created way even in this. We also are mysterious beings, incomprehensible to other creatures. This should give us a sense of respect and awe toward other human beings; it should warn us against thinking we have someone "figured out," or of limiting their potential, as we do when we think someone "will never change." This is not the problem, of course. The problem is when we hide ourselves deliberately, taking advantage of the admitted mystery within our hearts and using this shadow to hide our vices, or even our true selves, presenting only a mask to others. Even worse than this, and even more ridiculous, is when we think that we can be mysterious even to God.

Nowhere to Hide

It is not so with God. We may be mysterious to one another; we may be able to hide even from our dearest friends, but we cannot hide from God; we cannot fool him even with our most creative masks. We can even fool ourselves at times, but we cannot fool God. Psalm 139 begins thus:

> O Lord, you search me and you know me:
> you know when I sit and when I stand;

you understand my thoughts from afar.

My travels and my rest you mark;

with all my ways you are familiar.

Even before a word is on my tongue,

You know it, Lord, through and through.

But it is more than silly to think we can disguise ourselves before God; it is harmful. Our redemption depends on our coming to him honestly and openly, with trust and earnestness, and contrition. Bad theology leads by necessity to bad piety. When we admit who we are, and how we look to God, how he can read us as easily as we read a book, then we can turn to him and ask forgiveness:

Like an image engraved on a tablet, I am searched, O Lord, in my debts and sins which are written upon my skin and inscribed, and at all times shamefacedness hides my soul. O my Savior, be the absolver of my guilt, and have mercy on me.

The First Sunday of
the Victory of the Cross

The Lord will show forth his salvation.

You have showed your power among the nations.

In the hour that the wood of your cross was fastened, You shook the foundations of death, O Lord. And those whom Sheol had swallowed in their sins, Sheol released while trembling – your command quickened them, O Lord. Because of this, we also glorify you, O Christ the King:

have mercy on us!

May there not be grief upon grief for me

Lord, to you do I cry, O true Doctor: heal the wounds of my sins, for they crush me! If your grace does not stand before me, I would be already destroyed in so many evils. Cleanse my faults through mournful tears, and forgive my defilements in the mercies of your grace. O Christ, who has pity on all, pity me and have mercy on me, and turn me to you in your compassion. O Lord who loves his servants,

have mercy on me!

Sickness

Because human life is so precious, sickness is a serious thing. But unfortunately both of these facts are easy to forget when one becomes comfortable in his life. In good health, it is easy to neglect the sick; in the enjoyment of pleasure, it is easy to forget those around us. But at once take a step into a hospital, and the stark serenity of the place will remind one of both. The very air in the hospital is solemn and serious, demanding respect. Here we do not act as we do at a festival, though we rightly comfort the sick with levity. Here we do not feel as we do while at a party, though that may be our eventual goal in health. Someone is sick, perhaps dying, and everything else, every meager convenience or empty pleasure, is put aside and forgotten.

This is in the visible world; but what of the spiritual world? Is the sickness of the soul any less serious? Is it not much worse? Here it is not only the body which is hurt, but both the body and the soul. Sin is a darker, more harmful sickness than we can imagine, and the harm it does to our souls is beyond our guessing. The problem is not only that it is invisible; it is also somehow enjoyable. Sin is like a cancer that rips the soul apart while sedating it with pleasure, and so it can easily go unnoticed. The loftiest pride, which unravels our relationship with God, can be falsely justified. The most addictive lust, which rips our emotions to pieces, still has its attraction. The most blatant disobedience, satanic as it is, can be easily forgotten. Such diseases are covered up and protected by those who have them. Imagine someone with the flu hiding the fact so that no one cures him!

Indeed, sin is a harder sickness to heal because it requires our conversion; it requires that we admit our wrong, that we see ourselves as sick and turn to Christ who heals us:

Lord, to you do I cry, O true Doctor: heal the wounds of my sins, for they crush me!

Appreciation

Unfortunately, there is more. We can become so entangled in our sinfulness that even when we are healed, we forget our Doctor. Even after we admit our sins and turn to him for forgiveness, sometimes we return to our sins again, or, having received the healing we need, forget about the one who healed us. Such a healing is only partial, because the will is still wanders away and seeks a new sickness. No one leaving a hospital returns to life with full vigor; it takes time and patience to heal fully, and gradually health returns. In more serious cases, repeated visits to the doctor are necessary. Similarly, in the sickness of sin requires that we constantly return to our Doctor for his spiritual medicine. Without it, we forget him and lose ourselves:

If your grace does not stand before me, I would be already destroyed in so many evils.

Home

Christ is the true Doctor of our souls, and much more. He is not only our healing, but our very Life; he visits us not only to heal, but to remain. It is not like the sick person leaving the hospital and going home, who need never remember the doctors and nurses who care for him. Our continued health, our life in the Spirit of God, requires that the Doctor make his home within us forever, that we never turn away from him:

Cleanse my faults through mournful tears, and forgive my defilements in the mercies of your grace. O Christ, who has pity on all, pity me and have mercy on me, and turn me to you in your compassion. O Lord who loves his servants, have mercy on me!

The Second Sunday
of the Victory of the Cross

You have saved us from those who hate us.

Through the great suffering of the cross, you defeated
death, O Christ our Life-Giver, and became the
Resurrection and the principle of the rising of the
dead. You ascended in glory, and cherubim and
seraphim extol you upon the seat of glory. So with the
angels, we also glorify you, O Lord, and say: all that is
in heaven and on earth blesses and adores you, O
Christ our Savior!

And I, O Lord, hope in you.

While I adore you and confess that you are my Lord
and God, the enemy fights against me, and I am
buffeted by his battles. And as I cast him away by the
power of the Cross, he awakens my thoughts against
me, and through them he disturbs me. When he
entices my mind, and draws it away from you, he lays
traps for me and ensnares me, and with them he binds
me. And even when I run and take refuge in you, O
Lord, he runs and hinders me by the opposite path,
and confuses me with his guiles. Therefore, an earthly
being is unable to defeat a spirit without you. In you,
O Lord, do I take refuge, that in you I may win and he

**be defeated. No one calls to you and is deprived of the
aid of your grace. O Lord of all: glory to you!**

A Malicious Enemy

The devil is a being without mercy; he is an enemy that
cannot be bribed away, that is incapable of sympathy; even where
other enemies may desist when they have what they want, he has
no goal other than our destruction. We are often frustrated when,
even during prayer, or perhaps especially during prayer, the evil
one attacks us. "Is nothing holy to him?" we ask, "Can't he leave us
alone at least during prayer?" This is to expect too much of a
creature who has given his will totally to evil. On the contrary,
there is no better time for the devil to attack us than when we
pray; there is no decision we can make that is more irritating to
him, and so he lets loose all the hoards of hell to stop us from
speaking to our Creator.

Our Basilica Hymn for this Sunday begins with a sad
statement that is familiar to all of us who wish to dedicate part of
our day to prayer:

**While I adore you and confess that you are my Lord
and God, the enemy fights against me, and I am
buffeted by his battles.**

The Soldiers of Christ

St. Paul, in writing to Timothy, encourages him using military terminology: "Take your share of suffering as a good soldier of Christ Jesus." (2 Timothy 2:3). But the life of a soldier is not mainly in suffering; it is in fighting, as St. Paul writes later in the same letter: "I have fought the good fight." (2 Timothy 4:7). This fight is not, however, against any other human beings; it is against the enemy described above. Again, St. Paul (a master of spiritual warfare) makes this clear: "For we are not contending against flesh and blood, but against the principalities, against the powers, against the world rulers of this present darkness, against the spiritual hosts of wickedness in the heavenly places." (Ephesians 6:12).

The technique for this battle against the demonic forces of creation is a complex one, the details of which are found throughout Scripture and the Tradition of the Church. But our enemy would not be a worthy one if he were easily vanquished, or if he gave up without a fight himself:

And as I cast him away by the power of the Cross, he awakens my thoughts against me and through them he disturbs me. When he entices my mind, and draws it away from you, he lays traps for me and ensnares me, and with them he binds me. And even when I run and take refuge in you, O Lord, he runs and hinders

me by the opposite path, and confuses me with his
guiles.

The Humbling Conclusion

No, the devil does not allow us to go without a fight to the
end, and in the end we realize our weakness against so mighty an
enemy. Our hymn treats this reality almost in terms of a
syllogism, and makes an undeniable conclusion:

**Therefore, an earthly being is unable to defeat a spirit
without you.**

But this is not a moment of discouragement; on the contrary, it is
the very moment of salvation. The moment we realize our defeat,
our utter powerlessness in the face of the darkness fighting
against us, we can turn with all our hearts to the One who is alone
called the Savior. We cannot save ourselves by any personal
effort; it is Christ who must save us, it is he who is powerful
enough to defeat the devil. And so our hope is great, because even
after continuously losing to the devil, and, in some way, because
of our losing, we put our hope in Christ rather than in ourselves,
overturning the power of our enemy and using it against him:

**In you, O Lord, do I take refuge, that in you I may
conquer and he be defeated. No one calls to you and is
deprived of the aid of your grace: O Lord of all, glory
to you!**

The Third Sunday
of the Victory of the Cross

For the spring of life is with you.

The Cross of Christ became a spring for us, from which all our benefits gush forth: in it are demons defeated, and in it Satan falls; the power of error is abolished, sin is uprooted, deviation passes away, the boast of death, which had conquered our nature, fades, we accept, in it a spiritual birth, we dwell in immortal life, inherit the kingdom of heaven in his love, and take the appointment of sons of his glory. For Christ the King has taken the victory through his Cross, and made peace above and below. To him, with his Father and the Holy Spirit, do men and angels sing praise!

The light of my eyes was not with me.

From the weight of the roof of my offenses, the eyes of my mind have darkened from clarity, and I have strayed from the path of your commandments, which perpetuates life. I have made my journey in the way of destruction, along the path of the many, who inherit darkness and unquenching fire. Return me in your compassion, O Christ our Savior, forgive, in your grace, my offenses and my sins, and have mercy on me!

Night and Day

What do we mean when we associate "light" with faith and "darkness" with sin? Sin, for one thing, attaches us to itself; it is a kind of reverse-leech, enslaving us to the point where our feelings, bodies and minds are so attached to it that we cannot free ourselves by any effort of our own. This spiritual attachment to some one creature or pleasure can be described accurately as darkness, since in our eyes, eventually, the only thing that exists, the only thing visible to our souls, becomes our attachment, and everything else is forgotten, lost in darkness. For the universe to be obliterated in our minds and for only one object to fill our souls is to have the same spiritual darkness as Eve had at the moment of her temptation: "the woman saw that the tree was good for food, and that it was a delight to the eyes, and that the tree was to be desired to make one wise..." (Genesis 3:6). She saw the tree at that moment, and nothing else in the world.

This is the reality in which we first find ourselves as conscious human beings, and the farther we proceed in our sinfulness, the more we are enslaved to our attachments, the darker our minds and hearts become to the rest of the world around us, which God has provided:

From the weight of the roof of my offenses, the eyes of my mind have darkened from clarity...

Two Choices

The very ancient pagan world (before the time of Socrates, for example) and the modern world have one important thing in common: that is that neither believes in a true, objective "right" and "wrong." Instead, varieties of actions are described as different "lifestyles," and various objects of worship (things to which we willingly attach ourselves; idols) are described as "gods." Not so for the people of God. The book of Deuteronomy says this beautifully in the person of Moses: "Behold, I set before you this day a blessing and a curse: the blessing, if you obey the commandments of the Lord your God, which I command you this day, and the curse, if you do not obey the commandments of the Lord your God." (Deuteronomy 11:26-27).

In the New Testament, this reality is spoken of in terms of different "paths." There are not many, as in the modern or pagan world, but really only two: good and bad, light and darkness, God and satan. The latter path, to destruction, is unfortunately the easy one: "the gate is wide and the way is easy that leads to destruction." (Matthew 7:13). The former path, or way, is nothing other than Christ himself, for he calls himself "the way, the truth and the life." (John 14:6). But what do we do when we find ourselves off the path of Christ and on the wrong path?

...and I have strayed from the path of your commandments, which perpetuates life. I have made my journey in the way of destruction, along the path

of the many, who inherit darkness and unquenching fire.

One Way to Salvation

Christ is not only the Way for us; he is also the Good Shepherd who comes after us even when we stray from his path. He is the one who takes us upon his shoulders and brings us back to himself in his grace:

Return me in your compassion, O Christ our Savior, forgive, in your grace, my offenses and my sins, and have mercy on me!

The First Sunday of
the Crowning of the Church

O Lord, God of my salvation.
You give her peace and greatly enrich her.
O Lord, behold your Church, saved by your Cross, and your flock bought with your precious Blood, offers a crown of thanksgiving in faith to you, O High Priest of justice who has exalted her by your abasement. And, like a glorious Bride, she rejoices and exults in you, O glorious Bridegroom. In the strength of the Truth, raise the walls of her salvation, and establish priests within her, to be ambassadors of peace on behalf of her children.

A New Kind of Thing

The liturgical year is in some sense a study on the whole universe, from the mystery of creation to the most exceptional creature, man, to the man who is God, Christ, and all he did. This final season of the year, called "the Crowning of the Church," turns our sights not to the end of earthly time as did the season of the Cross, but to something existing both before and after that event: the Church. If creation is a mystery to a created mind such as ours, and if our won human nature is beyond our grasp since it is God's image, and if the Incarnation is utterly above our understanding, it stands to reason that the Church, which is somehow a combination of all these, is also a mystery we struggle to comprehend. Salvation history is the story of the encounter between God and man, and the Church is the culmination of that history: it is the place where man can meet God. Why this is the case depends on what the Church is, and on her relationship to Christ, who is not only the 'meeting place' between God and man in his own flesh, but who is both at once. All that the Church is, therefore, depends on who Christ is.

A Succession of Symbols

When one image is not enough to express an idea, an author is forced to move to another. This sometimes makes for weak poetry. But in the case of the Divine, it is easy to understand the need for mixed metaphors. The Gospel of John begins with a combination of many fascinating images used together: Word, Light, Life, etc. Christ himself is too much of a reality to be encompassed with a single image; the Church, therefore, must possess a similar characteristic. But because the Church only exists – the Church is only the Church – in relation to Christ, then any description of it we offer must include somehow not only a word on her, but also a word on how she relates to Christ, and he to her:

O Lord, behold your Church, saved by your cross,

The first defining thing about the Church, therefore, is that she has been saved by the cross of Christ – that is, by his passion and death. The same idea is enriched with another image:

and your flock bought with your precious Blood,

Now the Church is shown not only as an individual but as a collection – a 'flock,' which was purchased by the Blood of Christ. The response on the part of the Church (again, this is a matter of relation, which moves in two directions) is a particular type of thanksgiving:

offers a crown of thanksgiving in faith to you,

A crown is the reward given to a champion who has won a contest and the hearts of those watching, but here it is one of "thanksgiving," because by winning the contest the Champion has won not his own freedom but the freedom of the spectators, of those around him. This crown is given "in faith" because it is by this faith that we have access to the freedom won for us by our Divine Champion. The Church, then, is so far a flock being given salvation by her Shepherd, who is also the Champion with the crown. The next image:

O High Priest of justice who has exalted her by your abasement.

The image is taken from the letter to the Hebrews: "For we have not a high priest who is unable to sympathize with our weaknesses, but one who in every respect has been tempted as we are, yet without sin." (Hebrews 4:15). This gives insight into the role of Christ: he offers her this salvation by lowering himself for her; he can offer sacrifice to God on her behalf as her High Priest because he is near to her. Exactly how near he is to her is made clear in the next image, one which will become the predominant one for the rest of the Season:

And, like a glorious Bride, she rejoices and exults in you, O glorious Bridegroom.

The Lord is as close to the Church as a husband is to his wife – in fact, even closer, since husbands are told to look to Christ as their example (Ephesians 5:25).

Visibility

But the Church is no simply heavenly reality or mere idea or image. She is an earthly institution with flaws and enemies, and so there is a petition at the end of our hymn for Christ to:

In the strength of the Truth, raise the walls of her salvation,

We are not speaking, therefore, of a totally perfected and glorified Church, but of one still in need of prayer here on earth. The hymn ends with perhaps the most visible element of the Church, which again is revisited in later hymns during this season: the priesthood. The Church at the end becomes a mother, one with many children, children who need help and protection in this world:

and establish priests within her, to be ambassadors of peace on behalf of her children.

The Second Sunday
of the Crowning of the Church

Remember your Church, whom you chose from the beginning.
Indeed, I speak regarding Christ and his Church.
To your Church, O Savior, who has followed you perfectly by love and the faith which comes from baptism, you first showed the Persons of glorious Divinity; and through her, the perfect teaching of the mystery of the Trinity was revealed to the spiritual assemblies. By your grace, O Lord, may the creed that has been delivered to her by you in your Gospel be preserved without stain.

Sacramental Causality

In the prayer for the previous Sunday, we found that the Church has elements of both the spiritual and the physical, and there the spiritual and mystical flock and bride of Christ has concrete children and priests to take care of them. The priesthood, which is the class of servants of the Church, provides for the spiritual needs of the children of the Church in a highly visible way. The nourishment of the soul that comes about by receiving the Body of Christ, which is a heavenly reality, reaches the believer under the appearance of bread; the spiritual forgiveness which Christ effects secretly within the soul of the believer occurs through the audible words of the confessor; the very faith and love which are the spiritual foundations for the relationship between God and man, are the result, somehow, of baptism:

To your Church, O Savior, who has followed you perfectly by love and the faith which comes from baptism...

It is backwards to think that our faith establishes the Church. On the contrary, the Church, the mystical but still physical reality, is what provides us with our faith through her teaching and her sacraments.

Priority

Indeed, the Church is not only called the "Pillar of Truth," (1 Timothy 3:15), but in the first letter of Peter even more dramatic language is used: "It was revealed to them that they were serving not themselves but you, in the things which have now been announced to you by those who preached the good news to you through the Holy Spirit sent from heaven, things into which the angels long to look." (1 Peter 1:12). Through the teaching of the Church, we have something the angels do not have; or at the very least, it was from the Church that even the angels learned something of God. It was precisely through baptism – the baptism of the Lord by John the Baptist as well as the baptism he commanded his disciples to perform – that the teaching of the Trinity was revealed to the world. At the Lord's baptism, we have the voice of the Father saying "this is my Son," and the Holy Spirit descending like a dove and resting upon him. At the end of Matthew, the commission to baptize is the most explicit Trinitarian teaching of the New Testament: "Go, therefore, and make disciples of all nations, baptizing them in the Name of the Father and of the Son and of the Holy Spirit." (Matthew 28:19). It was through the Church, therefore, that first learned of the Trinity:

To your Church, O Savior, who has followed you perfectly by love and the faith which comes from baptism, you first showed the Persons of glorious Divinity...

Preaching to the Choir

The physical sacraments are not, therefore, any lower for being physical or embodied. The Son of God became flesh, became man, in order to exalt the flesh and unite it perfectly to his Divinity. It is no surprise, therefore, that even the angels of heaven were taught the depth of the knowledge of the Trinitarian God through the agency of the Church on earth:

and through her, the perfect teaching of the mystery of the Trinity was revealed to the spiritual assemblies. By your grace, O Lord, may the creed that has been delivered to her by you in your Gospel be preserved without stain.

The Third Sunday
of the Crowning of the Church

How lovely is your dwelling place, Lord God almighty!

That which God, not man, has established.

How glorious is your dwelling place, and beautiful your altar,

and great your magnificence, O Being who dwells in the

heights! The angels testify, who cry out and shout: holy, holy,

holy is the Lord who dwells in Light! The angels proclaim the

Trinity with their hallowings, as they say: glory at once to the

Father and to the Son and to the Holy Spirit! Grant us to

thank you along with them, and cry out to you with hosannas:

Great, O Lord, is the grace that you have effected for the

whole mortal race; O Lord, glory to you!

Solomon's Question

At a critical moment, Solomon, the son of King David, asks a critical question. David had desired to build the temple of the Lord, and had been denied the honor because of his transgression; but his son Solomon accomplished what his father could not do. Thus after generations of anticipation and years of work, the temple of Solomon was dedicated. It was during this dedication ceremony that Solomon asks his critical question: "Can it indeed be that God dwells with mankind on earth? If the heavens and the highest heavens cannot contain you, how much

297

less this temple which I have built!" (2 Chronicles 6:18). In the midst of an enormous celebration recalling God's presence among us in the temple, Solomon questions the very motive for the celebration!

But Solomon was only being a good theologian: how is it that God, a pure Spirit, can be in one place? It is a valid question, but not one without an answer. It is not a matter of God dwelling in one place and not in another, but of how he dwells in any particular place – or person. His presence in all of nature is real and powerful for those who seek him in his creation; but it is the presence of an Artist in his art. His presence in the temple was also real, and distinct from his presence in nature, since he had chosen this people to be his, and had himself commanded the building of the temple. His presence in the soul of a prophet must somehow be "greater," though there is no way for us to quantify how this is, than in an ordinary man, and certainly than in a sinner.

W-Miltha Bisra Hwa, W-Aggen Ban

In the Christian dispensation we find the ultimate presence of God and his true temple: Jesus Christ. In Christ, God dwells on earth not only as an artist or as the Lord of the Nation or even as one speaking through a prophet. In Christ God dwells on earth bodily, physically, in his perfect, complete union with human nature – with the man Jesus Christ. Nor did this earthly presence of God end when Christ was taken up to heaven, since the Holy Spirit, given by Christ, provides for his perpetual dwelling among us within the Church. This takes place through faith, which is the groundwork for any true dwelling of God on earth.

The Basilica Hymn of the Third Sunday of the Crowning of the Church takes up Solomon's question anew and examines it from the Christian perspective:

How glorious is your dwelling place, and beautiful your altar, and great your magnificence, O Being who dwells in the heights!

What exactly is the "dwelling place" and "altar" to which this hymn refers? This would be a simple question in the context of the season (that is, we could easily answer that God dwells in the Blessed Sacrament, which is on the altar during Mass), but the following phrases seem to confuse the issue:

The angels testify, who cry out and shout: holy, holy, holy is the Lord who dwells in Light! The angels proclaim the Trinity with their hallowings, as they say: glory at once to the Father and to the Son and to the Holy Spirit!

Even now, in the Christian world, Solomon's question returns: how is it that God can be in heaven, worshiped by multitudes of angels, and at once on earth?

Liturgical Completeness

Now, near the end of the liturgical year, is a time to reflect upon why the Church of the East has provided these hymns for the entire cycle. From *Subara* until now, there has been a deep meditation, every week, every day, upon the particular meaning of that time in the year. This has been in a larger context of the Prayer, as our Basilica Hymns are in the context of Ramsha or Evening Prayer. So we do not reflect alone upon the mystery of God's salvation, but together receive our meditation and our spirituality from our Church. But Ramsha is also in a larger context of the entire liturgical system of the Church of the East: it is combined with *Sapra* (Morning Prayer) and the other Hours; it is in the context of all the Sacraments, from Baptism on. Finally, all our reflection is within the context of the Holy Mysteries of the Eucharist, the culmination and high point of our worship of God.

It is there, at the Mass, that we find the solution to our Hymn's question, and to Solomon's:

Grant us to thank you along with them, and cry out to you with hosannas: Great, O Lord, is the grace that you have effected for the whole mortal race; O Lord, glory to you!

It is not only the "holy, holy, holy" of the angels in heaven (Isaiah 6:3) that completes the worship of God. No, this threefold "holy" is combined and intermingled with the "hosanna" of those dwelling on this little planet, those who saw the Messiah riding on a donkey and entering Jerusalem (Matthew 21:9, Mark 11:9, John 12:13). It is when the "holy" of the angels is combined with the "hosanna" of the people of God on earth that our worship of God becomes as perfect as it can be on this earth, and this combination is found at the beginning of the Eucharistic Prayer of the Mass:

Holy, holy, holy is the Lord God Almighty! Heaven and earth are filled with his glories! Hosanna in the highest! Hosanna to the Son of David! Blessed is he who came and will come in the Name of the Lord! Hosanna in the highest!

The Fourth Sunday
of the Crowning of the Church

For he is our God.

Listen, O my daughter, and see, and turn your ear.

Give thanks, O Church, O Queen, to the Prince who has espoused you and brought you into his summer home; and given you the dowry of blood that flowed from his side for you; and clothed you with the robe of splendid unending light, and placed upon your head the adorned and illustrious crown of glory; and, as with a pure thurible, has perfumed your scent before all; and, like a flower, blossoms and the buds of Spring has increased your radiance; and he freed you, on Golgotha, from slavery to idols. Therefore, adore his Cross, on which he suffered for you and exalted your lowliness, honor the priests who extol you with their works, and cry out to him: Glory to you!

In Conclusion

What does the liturgy save for the end? In this final week of the liturgical year, what is the image that we use to conclude and summarize all that we have reflected upon, from *Subara* until now? What is our conclusion, our ultimate goal in the life of grace? St. Paul tells the Corinthians the following: "I feel a divine jealousy for you, for I betrothed you to Christ to present you as a pure bride to her one husband." (2 Corinthians 11:2). The final image of the liturgical year, the ultimate reflection of our life in Christ, is that of the heavenly Bridegroom Jesus Christ and his bride the Church. No image is so abundant in Scripture – in both the Old and New Testaments – and so intimate and intense in its expression of how deep and dear is our union with God through Jesus Christ. St. Paul, again, writes to the Ephesians regarding the relationship between husbands and wives; how wives should honor their husbands as the Church honors Christ; how husbands should love their wives as Christ loves the Church and gave himself over for her; but his conclusion in this section shows that he is not merely giving practical advice to the married: "This is a great mystery, but I speak in reference to Christ and the Church." (Ephesians 5:32).

It is somehow the case, in a "mysterious" way, that the "true" Groom and Bride are Christ and the Church, and the earthly groom and bride are intended to be reflections of this heavenly reality. This is not the case with every image of Christ; we do not say that earthly shepherds are to be reflections of the heavenly Shepherd, nor that earthly doctors are merely shadows of the Divine Physician. But this image seems somehow to be a special case.

Cinderella

Our final Basilica Hymn of the year takes up this image and applies it with great creativity to Christ and the Church, showing beautifully how much greater is the love of Christ for his Bride than any earthly love:

> **Give thanks, O Church, O Queen, to the Prince who has espoused you and brought you into his summer home; and given you the dowry of blood that flowed from his side for you; and clothed you with the robe of splendid unending light, and placed upon your head the adorned and illustrious crown of glory; and, as with a pure thurible, has perfumed your scent before all; and, like a flower, blossoms and the buds of Spring has increased your radiance; and he freed you, on Golgotha, from slavery to idols. Therefore, adore his Cross, on which he suffered for you and exalted your lowliness, honor the priests who extol you with their works, and cry out to him: Glory to you!**

There are three sections in this hymn which subsequently deepen its theological tone: first, there is an introduction and expression of the wedding theme:

> **Give thanks, O Church, O Queen, to the Prince who has espoused you and brought you into his summer home.**

It is noteworthy that the first words are a command to show the Church how she is to respond to the indescribable gifts that are given to her.

The second section begins to make symbolic connections between the adornments of an earthly bride and the gifts that Christ has given to his Church:

...and given you the dowry of blood that flowed from his side for you; and clothed you with the robe of splendid unending light, and placed upon your head the adorned and illustrious crown of glory; and, as with a pure thurible, has perfumed your scent before all; and, like a flower, blossoms and the buds of Spring has increased your radiance...

As an earthly bride has a dowry, a dress, a crown, perfume and a bouquet of flowers, the Church has all of these things, but in a heavenly way: her dowry is the blood of Christ; her wedding dress is a robe of pure light; her crown is pure glory; her perfume is the incense of her Liturgies; her bouquet, amazingly, is spring itself, and all of nature, which is given over to her by the hands of her Husband and Creator.

The third section becomes totally explicit and leaves symbolism behind, but in doing so makes the previous symbols so much more potent:

and he freed you, on Golgotha, from slavery to idols. Therefore, adore his Cross, on which he suffered for you and exalted your lowliness, honor the priests who extol you with their works, and cry out to him: Glory to you!

Christ, on Golgotha, died for the Church, and in doing so freed her from the slavery of idolatry, giving her the freedom of true worship and union with God. Not only, therefore, is Christ the Bridegroom of the Church, but in his espousal, he has made the Church a Queen when she had previously been a slave. This is the primordial Cinderella tale – the tale of the lowly, sinful woman who was made pure and made royalty through the intercession of her Husband. But where the worldly bride has merely physical ornaments on her wedding-day, the Church has greater beauty and greater, spiritual gifts, coming from the side of Christ her Bridegroom and Savior.

Finally, the three commands given at the end of the hymn, which elaborate to the first command to "give thanks" which begins it, are: to adore the Cross of Christ, which is the instrument of her salvation and her freedom from slavery; to honor the priests who continue this mission of grace flowing from the side of Christ; and to praise her Bridegroom with all her heart and soul.

Made in the USA
Columbia, SC
24 February 2020